EARLY AMERICAN CRAFTS

AND HOBBIES

Early American Crafts & Hobbies

A TREASURY OF SKILLS, AVOCATIONS,
HANDICRAFTS, AND FORGOTTEN PASTIMES
AND PURSUITS FROM THE GOLDEN AGE
OF THE AMERICAN HOME

by

Raymond F. & Marguerite W. Yates

Edited by MARY LYON
Editor, *Craft Horizons*

Funk & Wagnalls
New York

FUNK & WAGNALLS PAPERBACK EDITION, 1974

COPYRIGHT MCMLIV BY
WILFRED FUNK, INC.

EARLY AMERICAN CRAFTS & HOBBIES
ISBN 0-308-10097-2
Library of Congress Catalog Card No. 54-9613
PRINTED IN THE UNITED STATES OF AMERICA

A Word to Hobbyists

Handicrafters looking for a change of diet will do well to consult this modest contribution. The authors wanted no more warmed-over dishes of hooked-rug weaving, soap carving, or ubiquitous potterymaking. Hence the last three years of their lives have been spent searching through the yellowing pages of *Godey's Lady's Book, Petersen's Magazine, The Glasgow Mechanics Magazine, The Ladies Wreath,* and ancient encyclopedias in an effort to unearth some of the crafts, the skills, and the hobbies that entertained our forebears before the days of the movies and the soap opera, and TV inroads on leisure time.

The search through the dusty old books, long since relegated to the storage cellars of libraries, brought forth some very interesting data, but that was only the beginning of the labors involved. Although not without compensating pleasure by any means, each old craft had to be tested anew and in many cases there was involved a diligent search for modern substitutes for many materials of an earlier day.

After much trial and error, and inevitable frustration, enough practical guidance was patiently assembled to warrant the presentation of our findings here. It is the earnest hope of the authors that it will serve to revive long-forgotten crafts which still have an enormous potential to stir the creative urge of those among us seeking some measure of escape from the problems of our day. Indulgence in pursuits, such as these, is not a guaranty of a complete banishment for the specter of the tax collector, the communist wood-borers in the Ship of State, or the prospects of atomic bombing, but it can surely help.

R.F.Y.

M.W.Y.

Lockport, New York

Acknowledgments

The authors gratefully acknowledge their indebtedness for the sympathetic assistance of the following people: Mr. Beaumont Newhall, curator of George Eastman House, Inc., Rochester, New York; Miss Bessom Harris, of Essex Institute, Salem, Massachusetts; Miss E. Florence Addison, of The Society for the Preservation of New England Antiquities, Boston, Massachusetts; Mr. Frank A. Taylor, curator, Smithsonian Institution, Washington, D. C.; Mr. Edward Warick, dean, Philadelphia Museum School of Art, Philadelphia, Pennsylvania; and Miss Rose T. Briggs, of the Plymouth Antiquarian Society, Plymouth, Massachusetts.

The Treasury

EARLY AMERICAN CRAFTS

AND HOBBIES

1. Typical silhouettes of the 1820's during the height of the "shades" craze, when America had hundreds of professional and thousands of amateur silhouettists. The lady's hair, left, was drawn with a fine pen.

Shades of the 1820's

{ 1 }

Among the most avidly collected antiques at the present time are the fine old "shadows" or silhouettes made in America between the years 1775 and 1845. Though the craft itself is very old, and there were a few professional cutters in the latter part of the seventeenth century, it was not until the beginning of the eighteenth century that the "shadow profile" became popular as a form of portraiture. At first accepted by those who could not afford a likeness in oil, it spread, in later years, to fashionable families who sought out the best of the "shade cutters" in England, France, and Germany; royalty, and even the highly sophisticated Goethe, succumbed. In his writings he tells us about making profiles of his family and friends.

The "shadow," the "shade," and the "profile" are terms now lost to the craft because of a penny-pinching French Minister of Finance under Louis XV. Etienne Silhouette preached national economy when extravagance was rampant. He soon became the butt of many French jokes, especially among the aristocrats who were having too much fun to worry over a situation that eventually cost them their heads. Silhouette's name was associated with anything tawdry and cheap: *"A la Silhouette!"* they cried derisively.

Although fashionable, the shade was regarded as a cheap substitute for a portrait in oil; hence, the derogatory term "silhouette." The name stuck and immortalized a man whose final indignity came in 1836, after his death. A committee of cynical French lexicographers voted unanimously to enter his name in the French dictionary as a common noun with its present connotation.

Lavater, a Frenchman who worked professionally at this profile art, was one of the first to improve on the earliest methods of silhouetting. First

3

among the problems to be met was that of a completely composed sitter. Even the smallest movement would so distort a profile as to make the result unrecognizable. The illustration of Lavater's so-called machine (I) shows how the subject was required to brace himself with his hands so that he should move as little as possible. Other silhouettists working with the same contraption took still further precaution by arranging a U-shaped device against which the neck of the sitter was pressed during a sitting. Lavater's arrangement of glass and translucent paper, so that he could work behind the sitter, avoided the interference of his own shadow which would have occurred had he worked between the light and the sitter. He used a pantograph for scaling. Although other more satisfactory aids were developed, the Lavater method can be used with equal success today, and can be simplified by the sitter's steadying his head against a doorjamb. The pantograph is still needed, however.

Chief among other silhouettists was Gilles-Louis Chrétien, a French artist, musician, and inventor. In 1786 he created his *physionotrace* which involved a reducing lens. The *physionotrace* was responsible for a large part of American historical portraiture. A French refugee, by the name of Charles Fevret de Saint Mémin, settled in New York City in the late 1790's

I. Lavater's famous 18th-century "shadow machine," which still offers a sound approach to the inexperienced silhouettist.

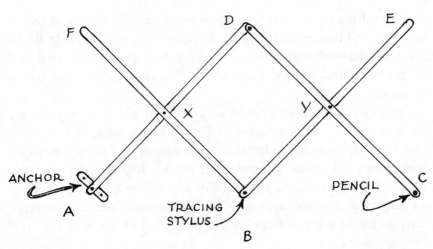

2a. How the pantograph operates. *AD* and *DC, FB* and *BE* are two pairs of sticks of equal length, hinged together at *D* and *B* respectively, and attached by screws at *x* and *y*. The apparatus is secured to a board or table at *A*, about which point it can be moved in any direction. Each of the sticks has a series of holes an equal distance apart; by setting the screw-hinges (*x - y*) in similarly numbered holes, the sides *Dx - By* of the parallelogram (*Bx - Dy*) may be made equal to, longer than, or shorter than the sides *Bx - Dy*. The longer *Dx* is relatively to *Dy*, the greater will be the movements of *C* relatively to those of *B*. If the reproduction is to be larger than the original, a pencil is inserted at *C* and a tracing stylus at *B*; if smaller, the positions are reversed.

and set up one of Chrétien's machines which he operated with great success until 1814. Exceptional skill made Saint Mémin's work a vogue, and few among the famous or the wealthy escaped his sharp pencil. More than a silhouettist, Saint Mémin was also an artist. He did more than just trace the profile of his sitter. In many instances the additional lines were drawn in with gold or silver ink, the finished product a true miniature. His production was prodigious, and hundreds of his profiles still exist in galleries, museums, historical societies, and private families.

August Edouart (1759-1851), master cutter of some 100,000 silhouettes, proves the subtlety of expression and artistic content possible in the craft. This gifted exponent shunned the profile machines and the technique of tracing; he stood before his subject, scissors in hand, and cut what he saw in duplicate from sheets of black paper.

During the 1830's, the years of his self-imposed exile in Bath, England,

Edouart's flying scissors caught the spirit of the times. Today the history of that town still lives in the hundreds of shades he created. Not only did his blades cut the swells and dandies of the town, but he walked the streets and caught the chimneysweeps, tin peddlers, shopmen, firemen, and leather dressers.

In New York City in 1839 he set up shop at 411 Broadway. During the next ten years he also worked in Boston, Philadelphia, New Orleans, and Saratoga, producing no less than 3,380 portraits and pictures of American citizens and scenes! So daring were the deft fingers of this artist that he didn't hesitate to record anything that appealed to him, whether it was an early locomotive and train or riding to the hounds. His sporting pieces were so full of verve and motion that the quality of his work has never been approached.

Many indeed were the professional silhouettists in America between 1800 and 1845, when finally the introduction of the daguerreotype emptied the studios of the shademakers forever and called the itinerant silhouettists in from the road. For years such men as the New Englander Moses Chapman had trudged the provincial byways of the country with their pack-a-back "machines" to record the shades of whole families for a few pennies each.

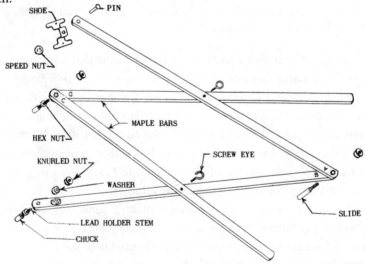

2b. Assembly of a purchased pantograph which carries two small chucks, one for pencil lead, other for a stylus. (*Courtesy Frederick Post Co., Chicago, Illinois*)

II. A specimen of the work of the master silhouettist Edouart, against a lithographed background especially printed for such purposes between 1825 and 1845.

In London at about this time, the early nineteenth century, Mrs. Harrington, who advertised that she "also cut with scissors," was using an optical device which did away with the pantograph. She used a box with a reducing lens and ground glass that had a mirror at a 45° angle inside. The image of the sitter was cast on the mirror, which reflected it upward onto the ground glass in the manner of the modern reflex camera. Mrs. Harrington placed a piece of tissue paper over the ground glass (working through a magnifier) and quickly traced off the profiles of her clients. As time went on, she became highly skilled in the business of tracing and filling in with black ink, and her customers were able to leave her studio within a few minutes carrying their "shades," as the English called them.

Most of us are not sufficiently adept at producing anything but caricature silhouettes freehand. However, if we turn to the use of a machine of some sort, there is no reason why we cannot produce very good likenesses of our families and friends.

3. Modern silhouettes of Kent and Lynn Wendel, nephew and niece of the authors, done by the old Lavater method. The originals are life-size.

4. Tommy Weeks, the little fellow next door. White ink has been used to draw in details of the clothing. Gold and silver ink was often used in the old days.

For simplicity, of course, Lavater's machine is not without merit. It is easy to make and easy to use. All that is needed is an old picture frame to hold a large pane of window glass measuring about 20 by 25 inches; a means of supporting it, either on a wooden stand, a pedestal, or in a doorway; and a piece of tracing tissue or other translucent paper stretched tightly and smoothly over the glass and held in place with rubber cement around the edges.

As the illustration of the Lavater machine shows, the sitter places his head within a few inches of the pane of glass. The light that is to cast the shadow on the glass and tracing paper is then moved either toward or away from the sitter until a sharp shadow is made. The size of the shadow may be adjusted by having the subject move closer to or farther away from the

III. A home-made model of Mrs. Harrington's "profile machine." For it the authors used an old focusing camera around which they set a cardboard box after removing the ground-glass back and installing it on the top of the box. A mirror mounted at a 45° angle inside the box reflects the image to the ground glass where it is traced on thin tissue.

glass. With this adjustment of the light source and the sitter, a sharply focused silhouette of proper size is achieved. Naturally, the best tracing is done at night with only one source of light. It is a help to put the light, an ordinary 100-watt bulb, in a photographic reflector. The tracing pencil should be very soft but also very sharp; use 00 sandpaper mounted on a wooden block for sharpening. The sharper the shadow and the sharper the pencil, the better the result in recording subtleties of character.

After the shadow has been carefully traced in pencil, remove the tissue paper from the glass and fix it to the surface of a piece of Bristol board with rubber cement. Then, to facilitate the reduction of the outline by means of the pantograph, trace the pencil lines with India ink.

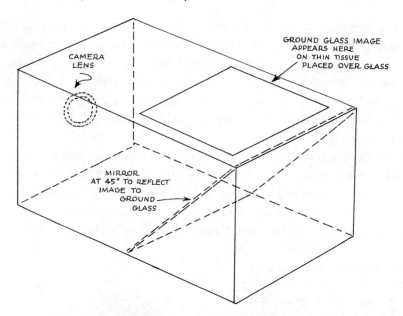

5. Operating principle of Mrs. Harrington's "profile machine." The size depends on the size of the camera from which the lens is taken. The lens from an old focusing camera is preferred. In this case, two telescoping boxes may be made so that an image of maximum sharpness will appear on the ground glass by means of good focus.

Invented in 1631 by a German, Christoph Scheiner, the pantograph was used extensively by silhouettists to increase or diminish the size of a drawing. While it is true that a pantograph (called a stork's beak in the old days) can be home-made, excellent finished products with graduated sticks can be purchased for less than $3 including full directions, at any stationery store. Purchasing instead of making is highly recommended unless you are mathematically capable of turning out a precision instrument.

The pantograph is quite simple to use. First decide how large the finished silhouette is to be, and set the pantograph accordingly. It was not the practice in the eighteenth and nineteenth centuries to produce large profiles. Rarely did they measure over 3 inches in height, and by far the larger number were much smaller than that, say more in the neighborhood of 1½ to 2 inches. Some of the finest examples of the more skilled workers measured ½ inch, or sometimes even less! However, you will quickly

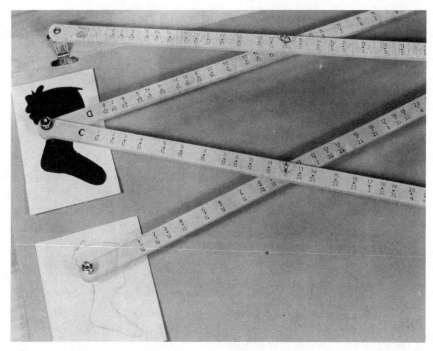

IV. A pantograph set up to trace a profile. In this way the profile may be made either larger or smaller.

V. Using a modern version of Mrs. Harrington's "profile machine," invented in England during the 1820's. The use of a magnifying glass is recommended for tracing small profiles.

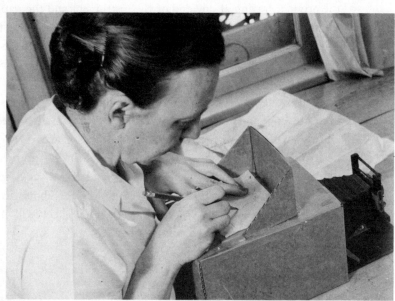

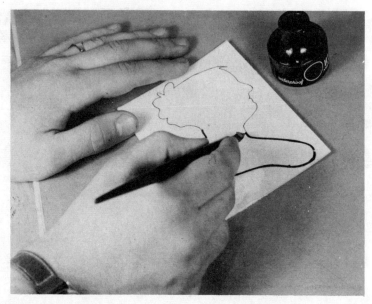

VI. Using a lettering pen to trace a silhouette outline before it is filled in with India ink. The tracing should be made just inside the pencil line but close enough to obliterate it.

discover your lack of tracing skill with the pantograph if you attempt to make your first tracings much smaller than 2 inches in height.

In setting up the pantograph, work on a table top in good light. Place the original tracing at one end of the instrument and the paper upon which the tracing is to be made at the other end, beneath the tracing pencil. Modern pantographs are equipped with small chucks made to hold leads such as are used in mechanical pencils. The leads used should have very sharp points—rub them over the oo sandpaper.

This done, trace over the outline of the original, and the pencil at the opposite end of the instrument faithfully draws a reduced or enlarged outline on the blank paper. Rough, "toothy" or absorbent papers should be avoided; they distort the outline. The thin board used for making patent drawings is of very high quality and has a good smooth surface. This material is available at stationery stores for about 20 cents a sheet and is very satisfactory for profile work. One sheet will make about 10 silhouettes of from 1½ to 2 inches high.

After the reduced tracing is made, do not attempt to fill it in with brush strokes immediately. Not many are skillful enough in the use of a brush to do this without producing at least a slight distortion of the features, and the greatest accuracy is necessary at this point. First draw a heavy line in India ink *inside* the pencil-traced line, using a No. 1 lettering pen. This line should be drawn close enough to the original pencil-traced line to obliterate it entirely. If the original tracing has been reduced to a very small size (the smaller it is, the greater the skill needed), work under a reading glass arranged on a stand. If you aspire to the best possible results, this is not a business that can be tossed off in a minute or two and without perfect steadiness of hand. Now go ahead and fill in the profile with your brush and India ink.

If you can lay hands on any sort of inexpensive camera lens and bellows, you can easily make a Harrington-type machine. The mirror can come from the 5-and-10, the ground glass from a camera shop (about 25 cents), and the box can be assembled from plywood or even heavy cardboard. Directions are given in illustration 5, although not dimensional details for the box because they will vary slightly with the focal specifications of the lens used.

If you choose to use cardboard boxes put together with glue and adhesive tape, make two boxes each with one end open and sized to telescope into each other. The lens may then be mounted and the lens box moved in and out of the other box until a perfect image or profile is cast on the

VII. A Saint Mémin profile miniature done in 1793 on the *physionotrace,* a machine invented by the Frenchman Gilles-Louis Chrétien. Saint Mémin worked his profiles up into actual miniatures. He was, however, a true artist and used the *physionotrace* only to increase his production. He did the portraits of many famous Americans while in New York City. (*Courtesy George Eastman House, Inc., Rochester, New York*)

ground glass. With such a focusing box, profiles of various sizes may be made. It is said that Mrs. Harrington's machine had sufficient scope to make profiles between 1 and 3 inches high.

In using the Harrington machine, good lighting and a good background will help. The lighting of the subject may be moderately bright, and the background should be plain white. For a perfect profile, you will need some sort of device to hold the sitter's head still—here, again, you might use the door frame.

The beginner will also discover that he cannot work without a magnifying glass of at least 3 or 4 power. The smallness of the image cast on the paper makes this absolutely necessary if results are to bear close resemblance to the subject. Remove the tissue-paper tracing from the machine and mount it on a piece of Bristol board or other suitable backing before retracing and filling it in with India ink. *It is imperative that a lettering pen be used under a magnifying glass.*

There were almost innumerable ways of handling a silhouette once the

VIII. Old daguerreotype cases make excellent mounts for silhouettes.

IX. A silhouette mounted on a plaster-of-Paris plaque.

tracing was perfected. While many silhouettists simply filled in their tracings, framed them, and let well enough alone, others developed all manner
of variations on the theme. The "hollow-cut profile" was versatile in that
it at once offered two likenesses of the same subject, each of which could
be used as it was or as a stencil. The tracing completed—but no filling-in
undertaken—the craftsman used a very sharp knife to cut out the form;
he then had the solid silhouette and also the "hollow."

Put it on black paper, on black or colored velvet or silk for a conven-
tional silhouette; use it as a stencil to produce many copies. Ink or fabric
of any color is suitable; not all old-time silhouettes were black. Some were
done in sepia, deep red, and other colors, although most of the cheap ones
made quickly by machine were simply traced and filled in with black.
Sometimes the hollow was used as a stencil on glass and the back covered
with gold leaf. The Swift Company, 1 Lover's Lane, Hartford, Connecticut
—for many years producers of high-grade gold and silver leaf—now have

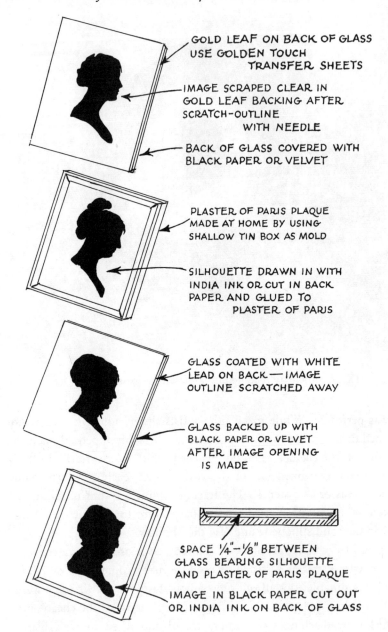

GOLD LEAF ON BACK OF GLASS
USE GOLDEN TOUCH
TRANSFER SHEETS

IMAGE SCRAPED CLEAR IN
GOLD LEAF BACKING AFTER
SCRATCH-OUTLINE
WITH NEEDLE

BACK OF GLASS COVERED WITH
BLACK PAPER OR VELVET

PLASTER OF PARIS PLAQUE
MADE AT HOME BY USING
SHALLOW TIN BOX AS MOLD

SILHOUETTE DRAWN IN WITH
INDIA INK OR CUT IN BACK
PAPER AND GLUED TO
PLASTER OF PARIS

GLASS COATED WITH WHITE
LEAD ON BACK—IMAGE
OUTLINE SCRATCHED AWAY

GLASS BACKED UP WITH
BLACK PAPER OR VELVET
AFTER IMAGE OPENING
IS MADE

SPACE ¼"–⅛" BETWEEN
GLASS BEARING SILHOUETTE
AND PLASTER OF PARIS PLAQUE

IMAGE IN BLACK PAPER CUT OUT
OR INDIA INK ON BACK OF GLASS

6. A few of the techniques of mounting silhouettes between 1800 and 1845. The appearance of the daguerreotype finally spelled the doom of the "shadow."

a product that even a child could apply. A form of transfer, it comes in sheets, is sold in art stores and paint shops, and is called Golden Touch. It is relatively inexpensive, and all you have to do is to soak the sheet in water for a few seconds, apply it gold side down and slip off the paper backing, leaving the deposit of 24-karat-gold leaf. The same applies to silver.

7. A silhouette of the first Anglican bishop of Virginia made during the 18th century and done without benefit of a tracing machine.

Artistry with the Camera Lucida

{ 2 }

When Captain Basil Hall, British naval officer and intimate friend of Sir Walter Scott, toured the United States in 1827-28, he brought along a new device, the Camera Lucida, which had been invented a short time before by the famous English chemist, Dr. William Hyde Wollaston. Using the Lucida, Captain Hall was able to make a fine series of sketches of Canadian and American scenes between Quebec and New Orleans. In 1829, Cadell and Company of Edinburgh published Hall's famous book entitled *Forty Etchings from Sketches Made with the Camera Lucida in North America*. Enthusiasm for the invention is indicated in the preface of Captain Hall's book:

"It adds greatly to the advantageous and agreeable use of the Camera to have a portable table as part of the apparatus. For this purpose, Mr. Dolland, instrument-maker in St. Paul's Church Yard, London, has recently devised a small brass frame which folds up, when not in use, so compactly as to stow away within the legs of a stand not larger than a walking stick. This, together with a camp stool of the same light description, renders the draughtsman quite independent of further assistance, especially if his instrument be furnished with the double movements, and other contrivances recently adopted by Mr. Dolland. With his Sketch Book in one pocket, the Camera Lucida in the other, and the sticks above mentioned in his hand, the amateur may rove where he pleases, possessed of a magical secret for recording the features of Nature with ease and fidelity, however complex they may be, while he is happily exempt from the triple misery of Perspective, Proportion, and Form,—all responsibility respecting these being thus taken off his hands.

"In short, if Dr. Wollaston, by this invention, has not actually dis-

18

covered a Royal Road to Drawing, he has at least succeeded in Macadamising the way already known."

Based on the principle of refracted light that projects an image through use of a prism of clear glass coupled with a mirror, the instrument is simple to construct and equally simple to use. With its help, anyone sufficiently patient and painstaking can outline a projected image on a piece of paper and can record accurately what is seen. This is especially true of scenery.

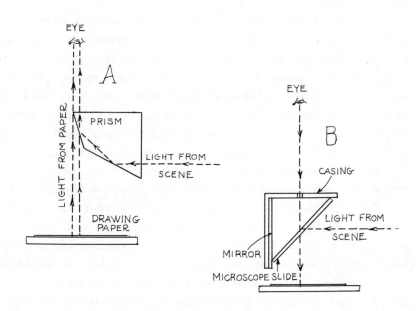

8. A. The optical principle of the camera lucida. The arrangement is here reduced to fundamentals. B. The prism of Wollaston's can be replaced by a small microscope slide and a mirror arranged as illustrated. This makes it possible for a home mechanic to make the camera.

To understand the operation of Dr. Wollaston's version of the instrument, it will be helpful to refer to A in illustration 8. (Don't be alarmed at the idea of having a special glass prism ground; it is not as difficult or expensive as might be supposed.) This shows that the eye must be carefully focused at the edge of the prism above the paper on which the sketch is to be made. When the eye is so focused, the worker sees the image or scene with one half of his eye and the paper below the prism with the other half. Therefore, the scene or object before the camera appears to be projected onto the surface of the paper. This is, of course, an illusion. Illusion or not, the thing is real enough so that one can accurately trace the outline on the paper with a fine-pointed soft pencil.

While it is conceded that Dr. Wollaston's invention is the best of all possible forms of the Camera Lucida, we must point out that an inexpensive substitute is easy to make and will serve in every way in which the Wollaston device was used.

Before attempting to build the more modern version of Camera Lucida, study 8B carefully. This will explain the optical principle employed and also the mechanical arrangement of the very simple elements involved. These consist of a small piece of good glass such as a microscope slide, a small piece of mirror, and a simple boxlike arrangement in which both these items are mounted, the microscope slide, about 2¼ inches long, at exactly 45° and the mirror, 2¼ by 2½ inches, directly behind. A peephole in the box-covering for the mirror and microscope slide is made directly above the slide. Other materials required for the instrument, illustration 9, include: a small iron or brass rod, ¼ inch in diameter and 12 inches long; a baseboard 5 by 8 inches; a metal washer with a ¼-inch opening; a machine screw or binding nut with a $1\%_{32}$ screw thread; and the material to construct the housing, which may be made of heavy cardboard, wood, or tin. In the latter case, the joints will have to be soldered. If you are clever with woodworking tools, there is no reason why you cannot fashion the housing from a single block of hardwood. Making the housing of either heavy cardboard or of wood will certainly simplify the problem of mounting both the mirror and the section of microscope slide. With either one of these materials, mounting may be done with model airplane cement.

A study of illustration 9 will show that the housing is closed at both ends but open on one side and on the bottom. Construction is simple and requires few tools. The ¼-inch metal rod is bent at right angles and with the dimensions indicated. It will be noticed that the metal washer with the ¼-inch opening is soldered to the horizontal section of the metal rod. This then functions as a shoulder against which the housing for the mirror and the microscope slide is gently pressed while the binding nut at the opposite end is tightened to hold the house in a precise position. In viewing some scenery, you may find it advisable at times to make slight adjustments in the position of the housing by this means. A second washer is slipped between the housing and the binding nut. This is not soldered to the metal rod, but is left free.

The horizontal portion of the metal rod used as a standard passes through the box holding the mirror and the microscope slide. So long as this rod does not pass directly beneath the peephole on the top of the box, there will be no optical interference.

If you do not have a $^{10}\!\!/_{32}$ tap with which to thread the end of the metal rod, you can have this done at a machine shop. If a $\frac{3}{16}$-inch hole is drilled in the baseboard (a small hardwood block, preferably maple) the metal rod can be driven into it with a forced fit. This should make for a permanent installation.

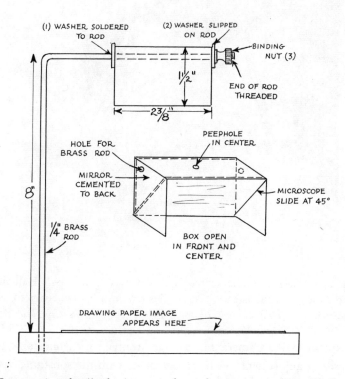

9. Construction detail of a home-made modern version of Dr. Wollaston's camera lucida.

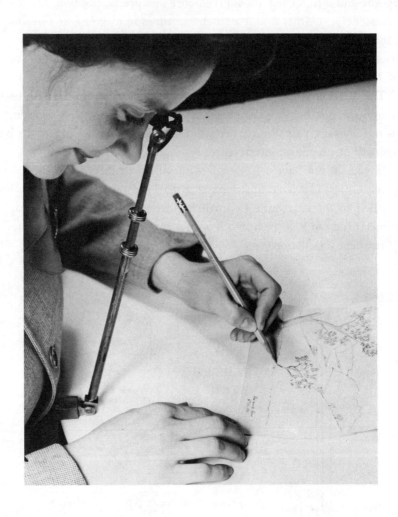

X. A camera lucida similar to the one used by Captain Basil Hall during his visit to America in the late 1820's; an illustration in his famous book describing his journey. (*Courtesy George Eastman House, Inc., Rochester, New York*)

Captain Hall's Camera Lucida was arranged with telescopic tubes for purposes of adjustment. Such arrangements with the substitute version are not necessary. Hall also mentions a clamping arrangement whereby his instrument was attached to the edge of his small folding table. The device

XI. Modern counterpart of the camera lucida made by the authors, using a small piece of mirror and a microscope slide as the principal optical parts. For the artistically inclined it offers many happy hours of relaxation.   XII. The home-made camera lucida in use. This little machine can be made in an hour or two at a cost not exceeding 50 cents.

just described needs no such refinement. When a tracing is being made, the operator uses his free hand to hold the base, thereby avoiding a clamping device. Use thumbtacks or rubber cement to fasten the paper to the base.

If you discover real enjoyment in the use of this device, you may want to set about designing and making a more permanent form of the camera. The instrument just described is suggested because its simplicity of design and materials bring its construction within the range of the kitchen table with a few modest tools.

On the other hand, those who want a true Wollaston instrument will find any optical house willing to grind such a prism for a few dollars. They will be able to do so by the aid of the sketch, 8A.

We warn you not to be too impatient if the scene or image before the device is not instantly discernible. In such a case, simply shift your eye about until a precise position is found after which the image will appear on the paper. If in using the instrument you fail to see the image after re-

XIII. When Captain Basil Hall of the British Navy stopped in the village of Riceborough, Georgia, he sketched this house with the then-famous new optical invention, the camera lucida. His travelogue was published in England in 1820 and bore the title *Forty Etchings with the Camera Lucida Made in America.*

peated relocation of the viewing eye, then resort to changing the angle of the viewing device itself. It is admitted that conditions can be highly adverse, but not to an extent that they cannot be overcome by a bit of trial and error. As you gain experience with the little device, the time will soon come when you will be able almost instantly to create the image on the drawing paper.

You may return from your vacation with a full photographic record of the scenes you liked and your newly discovered friends—wouldn't it be fun, also, to come back with a sketchbook filled with your own drawings? The little Camera Lucida will certainly offer you a new and quiet adventure.

XIV. Drawing made by one of the authors with the little device illustrated in 9 and 10, really a modern version of Wollaston's camera lucida.

Transparencies from Grandma's Day

Transparencies took many forms: painted pictures, designs, decalcomanias (transfers), and arrangements of dried flowers, leaves, or grasses. In any form, however, a transparency was mounted between glass or other transparent or translucent material and was hung where light, either natural from a window or artificial from an oil lamp, would pass through it. The inspiration for such work, obviously, came from the stained-glass windows of cathedrals.

During the early 1870's, many Victorian ladies whiled away their winter evenings with the new craze for making transparencies in the manner described by Mrs. C. S. Jones and Henry T. Williams in the book so popular at that time, *Making Household Elegancies.* A few years before, P. E. Vacquered had introduced in France his ornamental glass craft called *diaphanie* (really a transferable chromolithograph). Many American stationery stores sold *diaphanie* kits with which even the amateur could simulate stained-glass windows.

The *diaphanie* kits were relatively expensive. What with Papa earning eight or ten dollars a week and little Victorians coming along, such kits were a luxury. Hence the introduction of a purely American concept of glass transparencies that were perhaps more satisfying to sensitive people than the blatant colors of the French product. Certainly they were far less expensive and gave the hobbyist a greater opportunity to exercise her talents. The materials were readily available at the local stationery, drug, or hardware store, in the garden or field, and in the home.

The simplest and most beautiful of the transparencies of the 1870's involved carefully arranged flowers, ferns, leaves, etc., pressed between two panes of glass. Specimens were first prepared in a "botanist's press," illustration 10, which consisted of two flat hardwood boards pressed tightly together with binding screws. These transparencies were intended either for wall hangings or to be placed before a window. When they were made with a goodly portion of small, lacy ferns intertwined with other small-leaved plants such as baby's-breath, they expressed exquisite delicacy. They would still be in excellent taste in any modern house.

Victorian ladies made transparencies both with clear glass and with glass treated for a ground-glass effect. This is accomplished by covering *one* of the pieces of glass with a coating of clear varnish. As this is done, the glass must lie flat so that the varnish will not run.

While the application of varnish is reaching a tacky stage, a fine piece of Swiss muslin or tarlatan, cut to the same size as the glass, is laid on a flat, clean surface and given a coat of the same varnish with a clean brush. After both applications of varnish (on the glass and on the fabric) have reached a tacky or sticky stage, the fabric is placed on the varnished glass and pressed down gently with the fingertips to insure uniform contact at all points. This is essential for even lighting when the finished article is hung in a window.

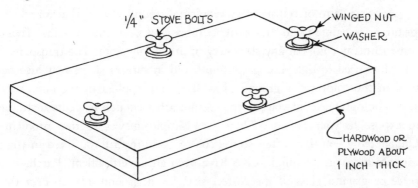

10. A home-made botanist's press, used by the Victorians to dry and press out specimens for use in the making of transparencies.

The time required for clear varnish to come to a tacky stage depends upon the warmth of the house and the degree of humidity. Modern varnishes usually require about three to four hours. (Clear lacquers may be used, but they will reach a tacky stage within a matter of minutes.)

After the varnish has set overnight, the dried, pressed flowers, ferns, or grasses are carefully arranged on the piece of fabric which has been previously attached to the pieces of varnished glass. A tiny dab of rubber cement may be needed to hold each specimen in place. You will, no doubt, wish to experiment with various arrangements before you use the adhesive. This accomplished, the second clear piece of glass is laid over the arrangement and the edges of the two pieces of glass are covered either with tape or colored ribbon. The problem in using ribbon is the possibility of the adhesive soaking through and causing discoloration. You may prevent this by first using the adhesive tape and then covering it with ribbon, using a small amount of rubber cement.

If you wish the ground-glass effect, you may have it without the trouble of placing the varnished fabric on the glass. Prepared ground glass, in sizes from 4 by 5 inches to 17 by 20 inches, is obtainable from any camera shop. It costs little more than ordinary window glass. Some of the Victorian ladies preferred perfectly clear glass. Window glass may be used for this effect, following the procedure already outlined but omitting varnish and fabric.

Another form of transparency requiring ground glass is that on which pictures are painted with transparent colored inks, such as Higgins. These come in many colors at any stationery or art-supply store. The transparent oil colors used to tint photographs and sold in camera shops may also be used in the coloring of ground glass. They are applied in the same way as to photographs. But you say you are not artist enough to paint anything to expose to your friends? There is a simple answer to that problem. Undoubtedly you have often seen a colored picture that you liked in your favorite magazine. It might even have been an advertisement. Purchase a piece of ground glass of the correct size, lay it ground-side up over the picture and trace the picture in light lines with a soft, sharp pencil point. Only a single piece of glass is used, as there is no need for a glass sandwich.

You then use colored inks to paint the scene with the original picture as a guide. The edges of the finished panel can be bound with adhesive tape and ribbon in the manner described earlier. Even though your drawing and painting ability has never progressed beyond the eighth-grade level, you should have a pleasing piece of work.

Using very simple drawings or designs, you can achieve a stained-glass

11. Floral motif of the Victorian ladies of the 1860's and '70's, drawn or traced on ground glass or glazed muslin, then painted either in transparent colors or opaque enamels. Very heavy black lines used with transparent colors simulated leaded glass. (From Jones and Williams' *Making Household Elegancies,* published in 1868)

window effect by using a lettering pen to go over the outlines of the design with heavy lines of India ink. Lines may be from $\frac{1}{16}$ to $\frac{1}{8}$ inch in width. A good example of the type of design suitable for such a technique is illustrated (11) which shows an urn of flowers in outline.

It is also possible to make charming transparencies on ground glass using the spatter technique described in Chapter 7. Ink of any color may be used, although black provides the greatest contrast. Pressed lacy ferns, delicate flowers, even sprays of grass will make effective displays if nicely arranged.

The ordinary decalcomania transfers found in paint shops may also be applied both to ground and to clear glass. These come in a wide variety of sizes and subjects and cost only a few cents each. If you wish, you may use

12. Popular motif used by Victorian ladies in creating glass transparencies so widely admired during the late 1860's and early 1870's. (From Jones and Williams' *Making Household Elegancies*)

the stained-glass effect and separate the various colors with a wide line of India ink. Not all "decal" subjects, however, lend themselves to this treatment. A panel or two of such lively coloring hung before a kitchen window will add a sparkling note; this is true with or without the application of India ink.

However they are mounted, transparencies may be hung on the wall or in the window with small brass wire rings attached to an adhesive-covered hinge which is applied to the back of the tape or to the ribbon covering it.

Our Victorian grandmothers and great-grandmothers were not only patient but ingenious, too. This is proved by a form of transparency that required the use of the steel engravings found each month in *Peterson's Magazine* and *Godey's Lady's Book* between 1840 and 1870. Up until the late nineteenth century, magazines and printmakers were limited to the use of woodcuts, lithographs (Currier and Ives were lithographers exclusively) and steel engravings—the latter were very expensive but still widely employed. You can find steel engravings in many old books and magazines: landscapes, seascapes, buildings, battle scenes (especially of the Civil War), and portraits. Many of the steel engravings in copies of Godey and Peterson are touchingly sentimental.

A simple technique for transferring these steel engravings to either ground or clear glass was practiced as early as the 1840's. Directions for this work, found in the pages of books long since yellowed and fox-marked, vary to some extent. The technique mentioned most often refers first to the softening of the ink on engravings by exposing it for several hours to a bath of turpentine. After such exposure, the print is removed and the excess turpentine is carefully soaked up with a clean blotter. The time required for this operation may vary, although forty-eight hours of exposure to the turpentine is usually sufficient. Before the engraving is removed from the turpentine bath, however, you should be ready to proceed immediately with the next step. This requires a few pieces of clean white blotting paper to soak up excess turpentine when the print is removed from the bath. It also requires a piece of prepared ground or clear glass of the correct size. To prepare the glass you must first wash it clean to remove all finger marks and grease spots, covering it with a coat of clear spar varnish after it has dried. The brush must be scrupulously clean; an old brush with particles of dried paint would cause trouble. When ground glass is used, the varnish is usually applied to the smooth, not the ground or frosted side.

The varnish should become tacky enough so that a finger will leave a print in it when only moderate pressure is applied. Here, again, the length of time required will depend upon the humidity. After the varnish has become tacky, the print is removed from the turpentine, blotted, and laid face down on the tacky surface. It should be pressed into this firmly and evenly. Then begins the process of removing the paper upon which the engraving was printed. This is done by gently rubbing with the fingertips —a process reminiscent of our school days, when we decorated wrists and notebooks with penny transfers. You must have a basin of clean water nearby into which you constantly dip the fingers of your working hand. You may need practice before you arrive at the correct pressure—just enough to roll away the moist paper without smearing the ink of the engraving which is attached to the tacky varnish. The procedure sounds a little more difficult than it is, actually.

In the old book *Making Household Elegancies* still another method of transferring steel engravings to glass is given. This calls for a mild soaking of the engraving between two pieces of clean cloth that have been placed in slightly salted water and wrung out. The engraving is left between the folds of cloth for several days until the moisture has thoroughly penetrated the entire surface. It is then removed and the excess water is blotted, after which the engraving is applied face-down to the previously varnished surface. Procedure from this point on is the same as in the directions outlined above. The cloth, of course, must be remoistened several times during the process.

To get really successful transfers, the job does not end here. You may, for example, wish to color the work. If the finished piece is intended for framing and hanging, color may be applied with ordinary oil paints or with household enamels found in the paint stores. On the other hand, if transparencies are to hang where they will intercept and transmit light, either natural or artificial, then the most delicate effects may be gotten by applying the color used for tinting photographs or with waterproof inks.

In regard to rendering steel engravings transferable, it may be pointed out that early workers did not use the method only on glass. In our collection of early nineteenth century hobby specimens we have several small wooden boxes with sides and lids decorated by transferred steel engravings. That this old decorative craft had its beginning well over a hundred years ago is proved by the date and the name of the hobbyist under the lid of one of the boxes. The inscription indicates that "Watson made this box in 1832." As might be expected, a number of the transfers show Lafayette, Washington, the American Eagle, Webster, and the American Indians. A still flawless (save for slight yellowing) coat of varnish has effectively

XV. Transparency produced on ground glass and painted with colored water-proof inks. The leaded glass effect is achieved by outlining the object and the border panels with India ink and a lettering pen.

XVI. An old engraving transferred to an antique clock glass by the authors. After old steel engravings are soaked in turpentine, the ink usually softens sufficiently to adhere to a tacky varnished surface thereafter.

preserved these transfers over the hundred and twenty years that followed their application by Watson.

Regardless of the nature of the surface to which steel engravings are transferred, it should be covered with a thin coat of spar varnish immediately after the transfer has dried, which will take at least forty-eight hours. A proper mixture is one part varnish, as it comes from the can, and one part turpentine.

When engravings are applied in this manner to parchment or very heavy parchment-type paper, they make attractive lampshades. Your local printer will order this special, though inexpensive, paper that comes in sheets large enough for a good-sized shade. The paper should be held, by thumbtacks, flat to the surface of a board while it is being worked on. After the engraving has been transferred and allowed to dry, a thin India-ink line can be drawn around its border and, outside of this, a slightly wider line. Then the whole shade is given a coat of thin spar varnish, diluted as mentioned.

Although lampshades decorated with plain black engravings are most effective, there is no reason why these transfers should not be in color. The oil-base colors used for tinting photographs are ideal for this purpose. They are applied in the same manner as that recommended for photographs: that is, with a small piece of cotton batting. This should be done only after the engraving is perfectly dry and hard and before the final protecting coat of spar varnish is applied.

XVII. A piece of late-Victorian tinselwork from the author's collection of old-time artcraft specimens. Directions for producing such work are given in the next and in illustration 13.

Still another form of transparency evolved during the latter part of the Victorian era, one used almost exclusively for folding screens. We have seen only two examples of this work in our twenty-odd years of delving into the hobbies of the Victorians and collecting representative specimens. While all transparencies discussed before were made on glass, this one involves a special preparation, applied to fine muslin. It makes the muslin stiff and translucent. The preparation of the gelatin sizing that is needed is easily made in the kitchen. The gelatin is dissolved in a little cold water. Then a very small amount of hot water is added to dissolve any tiny globules which may remain and which would produce a bumpy surface. We found in old directions the admonition to have the mixture about the consistency of thick cream, but with modern gelatin we discovered that a thinner mixture works better, even though a few more coats must be used. This mixture is repeatedly brushed or painted on the muslin, which must be held taut in a wooden frame. This can be done by cutting the muslin about 1½ inches oversize and holding its edges tight to a wooden frame by means of thumbtacks. Five or six applications of the sizing will be needed on each side of the muslin. Each coating should be allowed to dry completely before another is applied. (You will find a bowl of hot water useful in regulating the thickness of the gelatin sizing. If the mixture threatens to become too thick, placing it over the hot water will soften it to the proper consistency.)

After the last coating has dried, the muslin is removed from the frame. The gelatinized surface will not only be hard, but displeasingly glossy, too. This gloss will have to be reduced in the following manner: First, with thumbtacks, hold the muslin flat and taut on a table top. Some stretching is required, since the fabric should be without any wrinkles. Then use fine steel wool to rub the whole surface with moderate pressure and a rotary motion for an even texture. Just enough cutting of the surface in this way is required to produce a sort of mat effect. You then use a clean, damp cloth to pick up the gelatin dust that remains on the surface. Since both sides of the muslin are gelatinized, both sides must be treated with steel wool.

XVIII. *Right.* A document box dated 1836 decorated with steel engravings obviously taken from the books of the day. These engravings are not merely pasted on, but actually transferred by the process outlined here.

If you draw your own design or scene on the gelatinized surface, you will need only a soft drawing pencil. Or, you may wish to take advantage of an old trick of the Victorian hobbyist. Say you select a suitable design (a floral group, for instance) from a piece of wall paper. The design is first laid on a soft board (a piece of composition board is excellent) and the outline of each part formed with a series of punctures—about ¼ inch apart—made by a large darning needle. This done, the design or scene is placed on the muslin.

What is known as a pounce bag is used to sift a fine powder through the holes in the paper so that when the paper with the design or scene is removed from the gelatinized surface, a series of tiny spots of powder are left. These are then simply connected with marks from a soft pencil to reproduce the scene or the design that was on the needle-pricked pattern.

A pounce bag is nothing more than a piece of cotton cloth used as a bag for powder fine enough to sift through it. The powder may be of any color so long as it provides good contrast. This powder (say an ounce of it) is piled up in the center of a piece of cotton about 4 inches square. A small bag is made by wrapping the powder in the cotton square and tying the top with a piece of string. When the bag is gently pounced over the darning needle holes that outline the picture or design, some of the powder sifts out and falls into the holes, thereby marking the surface beneath with tiny dots. After the points are connected with pencil lines, the remaining powder may be brushed away.

Muslin prepared in this way may be colored variously, provided the coloring matter is transparent. Beautiful pastel effects are available for tinting photos. Sharper, more blatant coloring can be achieved with waterproof inks. Even the transparent oils may be used. In any event, if lampshades thus decorated and colored are to be made practical and washable, they must be covered with water-white varnish. Two coats, each applied in a dust-free atmosphere, are better than one.

Although, strictly speaking, not a form of transparency, the tinselwork done by Victorian ladies during the Civil War years might be mentioned here. This was done on glass with transparent colors. It was a popular hobby, many excellent examples of which still exist. If executed with care and a degree of talent, tinsel can be charming. Much depends upon the worker's dexterity, his sense of balance and color, and his ability to paint

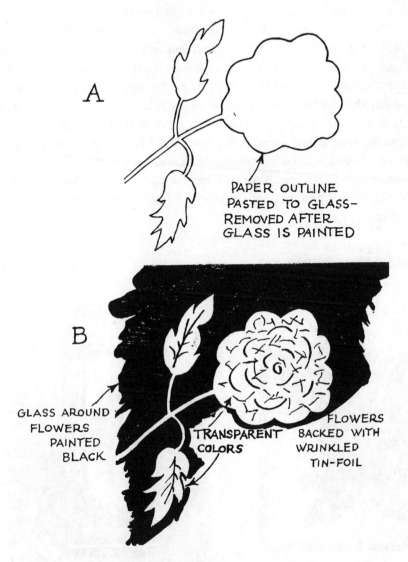

13. Principles involved in making tinsel pictures, a hobby that thrived during the 1860's and early 1870's. The flowers, birds, or other designs are first cut out of paper (*A*) and pasted on clear glass. The glass is then coated with dull paint or glossy enamel (worker's choice) and the paper is removed, leaving a clear opening in the glass. These openings are then filled in.

flowers or birds or whatever. A sample of this work is shown in XVII.

To produce tinselwork, you must first cut the outlines of the flowers, birds, or leaves of your design in paper and affix these to the surface of the glass with rubber cement. Then the uncovered portion of the glass is coated with ordinary black enamel (13). After the enamel is dry, remove the cutouts and rub away the remainder of the rubber cement. This will leave blank or clear spaces into which you paint with transparent colors the flowers, buds, stems, doves, or whatever you have chosen. You then place pieces of wrinkled tinsel or aluminum foil in back of each flower, bird or leaf, crushing it in your hand and then flattening it somewhat. As backing in the glass it reflects light through the transparent colors used for the design.

XIX. Two samples of glass transparencies of the 1860's. The piece at the left was intended to be hung in front of a window and involved botanical specimens pressed between clear or ground glass. The article on the right was made in the same manner and was called a "lamp screen." (From Jones and Williams' *Making Household Elegancies*)

A Touch of Charm:
Design Your Own Wall Paper

{ 4 }

When Michael Perry, Boston bookseller and stationer, died in 1700, the inventory of his worldly possessions included "7 quires and 3 reams of painted paper." Perry numbered among his clientele at the time many of the wealthy people of the Bay Colony who could well afford to decorate their walls with fashionable and expensive coverings. Although called "painted" paper, it was really stenciled paper that had been introduced in France by François of Rouen in 1620. It was a substitute for the more expensive tapestry and silk hangings in vogue among the French aristocracy. The idea had been introduced to England and thence to the Bay Colony, where its vogue continued into the early years of the nineteenth century.

First sold in sheets measuring 22 by 32 inches, the paper was applied by means of paste, just as it is today. Later these sections were joined into 12-yard lengths and sold in rolls. Unfortunately, the rolls were so costly that only the wealthy could afford them. Yet there were few of the fashionable first houses on Beacon Hill in Boston that did not boast one or two rooms hung with these papers.

During the early days of the vogue, paper stainers, as they were called, used stencils of cardboard for transferring their designs. Later, cut blocks of pear and sycamore wood were used, as was done for handprinting of calico. A great deal of it was imported from England but, as demand grew, a few colonial craftsmen entered the field and established an industry that thrived for many years. However, the craft was not limited to stenciling wall paper. Those who emulated the rich were not to be outdone because they could not afford such luxury. George Killoup's advertisement in the Boston *News-Letter* of 1768 informed the "gentlemen and ladies of the towne and country that he paints carpets and walls and papers rooms in the neatest manner and will take English or West Indian goods as pay." The direct stenciling of floors and walls was popular in America until the 1840's. Examples of this work survive today in many neo-classic houses of the 1830's.

As for the stenciled paper, both early and late, many charming samples have been handed down. Some of these have been discovered buried under the paper coverings of New England houses, and many of the 1800-1825 period have been found on homemade covers of old almanacs. A large number of these papers have been preserved by the various antiquarian societies of New England.

Some idea of the variety of designs used during the 1790's may be gathered from the advertisements of the period that mention "Brocade, velvet and chintz figures, flower pots, festoons, variegated paper on the subjects of war, peace, musick, love, rural scenes, etc. as produced at the manufactory of Joseph Hovey at his paper-staining and calico-printing establishment at No. 39 Cornhill, near the market, Boston."

Those who wish to try this craft will be delighted by the simplicity of

14. A late 18th century advertisement of one Ebenezer Clough, "paper stainer" of Boston. All early American wall paper was decorated by hand in the simple manner described in this chapter.

15. Authentic 18th-century design for stenciled wall paper.

the technique and the availability of inexpensive materials. Plain background papers of varying quality can be bought at any wall-paper store. The stencils are far easier to apply than those used for furniture decoration; and any of the new water-soluble, rubber-base paints—Super Kem-Tone, for example—is virtually made to order for such work. There must not be any natural oil in the coloring matter, for if oil-bearing paints or enamels are used, the oil will bleed onto the paper at the edges of the design and produce a disastrous effect. The water-thinned casein paints are excellent for stenciling wall paper, and any of a thousand shades can be mixed by using standard color pigment. These are simply stirred into the already-prepared paint.

Ordinary stencils are used for the application of the paint to the wall paper. If a single color effect is sought, then only one simple stencil is needed. This is cut in the same manner as the stencils used in decorating furniture (See Chapter 12). The design, which may be a flower or cluster of leaves, is drawn upon stencil paper and cut out with a very sharp knife—sharp enough so that no fibers protrude after the cutting. Clean-cut edges that make for good stenciling are essential.

Paper used for stenciling must be tough and strong. In preparing enough stencil paper even for a small room, since the design is to be repeated many times, it must be able to withstand much handling. You should buy regular stencil paper at a paint shop. If this is impossible, then a heavy, tough type of craft paper may be used, and after the design is drawn in, it should be soaked in melted paraffin. This will make the cutting out of the design easier.

It is apparent that where two or more colors are to be applied to wall paper by this method, a separate stencil may be necessary for each color—for instance, in the case of a red tulip with green leaves and stem. One stencil may be needed for the blossom and one for the leaves and stem. However, if the elements of a design are far enough apart so that two or more colors may be applied without danger of mixing the paint, only a single stencil is necessary. This will not be the case with small, intricate designs.

Fortunately, the synthetic paints are fast-drying and will set within a few hours' time. To facilitate both handling and drying, the paper may be pre-cut in lengths slightly longer than the distance between the ceiling and the baseboards of the room to be papered. When the paper is ready for drying, it may be stretched out on the floor or draped over furniture or temporary wooden racks, made ready beforehand, or it may be laid out in an unused room or in the cellar or attic.

Stenciling should be done on a solid surface. A large piece of 5/8-inch plywood (say, 3 by 8 feet) placed on three sturdy horses will supply an excellent worktable.

Geometrical problems also have to be considered. No set rule can be

16. Another example of authentic 18th-century stenciled wall paper as produced by the "paper stainers" of New England. Such work is now easily duplicated at home with the aid of modern materials.

determined because each job is an individual challenge. But the problems do arise both in the printing and in the appearance after the paper is on the wall. In any event, each roll requires careful distribution of the pattern. This is easily accomplished by blocking off sections with light pencil lines that may be easily erased. The size of the sections and whether they will be square or oblong depends upon the size of the design and the distance between each application of the design. Whatever the size of your piece of wall paper, block it out in equal sections and apply the design to the exact center of each section.

For example, if a section 6 by 6 inches is needed for the application of the stencil, cut a piece of cardboard 6 by 6 inches square and punch a small hole in the exact center of it. Starting at one corner of the paper, lay the cardboard in place, outline it faintly with a sharp, soft pencil and make a dot through the hole in the center. Move the cardboard to an adjacent position, using the pencil line as a guide, and continue blocking the wall paper until the entire piece is laid out, indicating the positions for the stencil.

In applying paint to the stencil, one of two devices may be used, but the most important single factor is to avoid using too much paint. Either a regular stencil brush (shown in XX) or a small piece of clean sponge is serviceable. If a professional stencil brush is used, dip only the tip ($\frac{1}{8}$ to $\frac{1}{4}$ inch) in the paint, wipe off excess paint on the edge of the can, and use the brush vertically with a stamping motion.

Only enough color to insure complete, uniform coverage should be applied. While applying the paint, use your free hand to press the cut-out edges of the stencil firmly against the paper. It is essential to prevent the paint from seeping under the edges of the stencil, destroying its sharp outlines. This will not happen if the brush or sponge is never overloaded with paint. It is far better to dip into the paint pot repeatedly than to risk too much paint at any time.

There is no reason why stencils may not be applied directly to plastered walls. Before doing this, however, first cover the walls with a washable flat or semi-gloss paint—either white or an appropriate pastel. The geometrical distribution of the design on the wall is little more complicated than on wall paper. Pencil guide lines may have to be omitted, however, because they cannot be as easily erased from plaster as from paper. The cardboard, used to block wall paper, is still useful here, although only the center dot is marked with pencil. Put a very small hole in the center of the stencil and place that hole over the pencil dot from the cardboard.

A novice may have trouble at first in lifting his stencils from freshly painted surfaces without leaving a slight smear. It takes very little to destroy a good sharp outline. A steady hand is a help. Also, dog'searing two corners of the stencil makes it possible to get a firm hold on it and to lift it *straight* up.

Stenciled walls, whether covered with paper or plaster, can be contemporary and in vogue. We do not need to hold to the quaint old designs and motifs; the whole world of design, antique and modern, is open to the worker. Only the method is ancient. You would like a design involving a space rocket? Why not? This is just as easily produced as a design for an early-Victorian room or a room with Sheraton, Chippendale, Hepplewhite, or Duncan Phyfe furniture.

For a number of years now, R. E. Thibault, Inc. of New York City, has

XX. Stencil, paint, brush, and a sample of home-stenciled wall paper made by the authors. The text makes clear the manner in which this interesting and rewarding hobby can be accomplished for attractive home decoration.

XXI. Stenciling plain white wall paper with a water-thinned casein paint and a special stencil brush. If such a brush is not available, color may be daubed on with a piece of sponge.

been reproducing authentic designs of early American wall paper. They have combed New England thoroughly for the most appealing specimens of the old craft, and their research has brought rich rewards. Penciled outlines of two of the designs chosen by this house are shown in 15 and 16.

If you wish to dig more thoroughly into the subject of the stenciled papers, walls, and floors of the period between the years 1700 and 1840, there is an excellent book by Janet Waring, *Early American Stencil Decorations*, Century House, Watkins Glen, N.Y.; copiously and elaborately illustrated, it is a source of authentic information for those who wish to master more completely the decorative essentials of this fine old American craft.

During the last half of the eighteenth century and the first twenty-five years of the nineteenth, many fine pieces of scenic, block-printed paper arrived in America, mostly from France and England. A very costly material, it was produced in many colors by means of printing blocks cut from such close-grained woods as pear, box, holly, bass, maple, or gum. The designs, or scenes, were drawn directly on the wood and then carved out. The wooden blocks themselves were about 1½ inches thick. In actual use, the printing surface of a block was covered with ink, then laid face down upon the paper in the proper positions. The block was then struck a sharp blow with a mallet.

Provided that the craftsman keeps to simple forms and uses no more than two colors, there is no reason why wall paper cannot be printed in this manner, using ordinary printers' ink. Persons of talent and experience might even print scenes involving the use of seven or eight blocks, each with a different color. As in printing with linoleum blocks, the ink is applied to the block first by laying it on a piece of glass, rolling it out, and using a small rubber roller to ink the block.

XXII. A sample of the costly hand-printed wall paper made for the American trade and imported from France during the early part of the 19th century. The printing was done with wooden blocks. (*Courtesy Essex Institute, Salem, Massachusetts*)

HAND-PRINTED FROM THE ORIGINAL WOOD BLOCKS

BY
J. ZUBER & CIE

Antique India Painting for Modern Homes

{ 5 }

This is a craft which is easy to master and pleasing in its results. Victorian ladies of the middle class developed India painting as a substitute for the expensive ivory-in-ebony inlay work that only the wealthy could afford.

This form of painting was actually a reversal of stenciling. The stencil involved paper cutouts of leaf, flower and fruit shapes, which were laid over surfaces to be decorated and were filled in with paint and metallic powders. India painting involved paper cutouts of similar or identical shapes which were pasted temporarily to the object to be decorated and then the whole surface was covered with black paint. After it dried, the paper cutouts were removed, leaving the space beneath in the natural wood color. Thus, a sort of reversed silhouette remained. Sometimes solid reds or blues were used in place of black; there is nothing to limit the variety of color. An examination of illustrations 17 and 18 will give an excellent idea of the methods used and the finished effects.

This technique was used for decorating small wooden boxes, chess boxes, borders of chessboards, edges of wall shelves, wall plaques, and even fire screens with gelatinized muslins as described in Chapter 4. One also discovers, though rarely, relics of glass decorated by the same means.

Wood was the most widely used background. With ebony, an almost black wood, the process was modified. To simulate an ivory-inlay effect, the craftsman pasted an ordinary stencil over the surface of the wood and painted with ivory-colored paint or enamel in the cut-out surface. When the stencil was removed, leaves and flowers or other motifs were in solid ivory surrounded by the natural ebony. Dark mahogany called for the same treatment.

On the other hand, when very light-colored woods, such as white pine, beech, or poplar were used as background, solid cutouts of the motifs were pasted to the surfaces, black or other paint was applied over the whole surface, wood and paper alike. The removal of the paper, after the paint had dried, left a black background with the flowers and leaves in the natural color of the wood.

Sometimes boxes were made of Bristol board instead of wood. The modern hobbyist can make these in any color, since Bristol board offers a wide range of selection. Offhand, one may suggest a delightful combination of dark green background with yellow Bristol board showing through. Such effects, however, cannot be achieved by the use of oil-base paints. The highly absorbent Bristol board will tend to draw the oil out of the paint and allow it to bleed into the unpainted sections. The effectiveness of all forms of India painting depends upon very sharp outlines which the oil may destroy. When Bristol board is used for India painting, colored lacquers or a rubber-base paint must be used.

The same is true, to a lesser degree, of the softer, open-grain woods such as white pine and beech. To eliminate the bleeding hazard completely, it is wise to cover the wood beforehand with water-white varnish (a perfectly clear varnish available at any well-stocked hardware store). Pre-treatment of the natural wood surface will pay off handsomely in final results. The hobbyist may also use colored lacquers if he prefers.

Sharpness of outline, a must for a finished appearance, can be further insured by using a very sharp knife on the cutouts. A lightweight grade of stencil paper as supplied by paint stores gives the best results. The knife should be honed repeatedly to insure an edge that will cut and not tear the stencil paper. A dull knife will leave uncut paper fibers at the edges, and these produce fuzzy outlines.

Another way to secure sharp outlines in the finished work is to fix the paper very carefully to the surface of the article to be painted. Nothing is better for this purpose than rubber cement. It is imperative that the edges of the paper be attached securely. Otherwise the paint or lacquer will ooze beneath them and destroy outlines.

After the paper is covered with the cement, it should be exposed to the air for a few minutes while the excess solvent evaporates. This insures maximum adherence. The paper is then laid, cement-side down, on the surface of the object. The fingertips then are pressed hard on all edges to

17 and 18. A checkerboard and a handkerchief box decorated with the so-called India painting of the 1870's. In the case of the checkerboard, cut-out paper was used. Natural leaves, however, were used to produce the uncovered spaces on the handkerchief box (page 52). India ink was used later to draw the veins of the leaves and other such details.

effect a paintproof or lacquerproof seal between the wood and the paper cutouts. But be sure no rubber cement remains at the edges of the design.

After the paint or lacquer has dried, the paper should be removed immediately to insure a minimum of trouble. If rubber cement is allowed to set too long, it becomes increasingly adhesive. The small deposit of cement left after the paper is removed can be easily rolled away with the tips of the fingers. Since most workers prefer to give all finished work an overall covering for resistance, it is advisable to remove every trace of the rubber cement. This can be done with a very light application of fine steel wool followed by a careful wiping with a damp cloth.

Because an application of ordinary amber-colored varnish tends to dull the over-all effect, a water-white varnish is recommended. After this is completely dry, it may be treated again lightly with fine steel wool, then waxed and polished. Any good grade of furniture wax will give the effect of an enameled surface.

If you have access to a vacuum cleaner with a spray gun, you can approach the project more easily. Natural leaves, maple or fern for example, may be fixed with rubber cement to the surfaces to be decorated. Then several very thin coats of paint, colored varnish or lacquer may be applied with the spray gun. After drying, the leaves are removed. Thus, the bother of making paper cutouts is avoided. Talent for this method lies in the hobbyist's ability to arrange the leaves in an effective manner. The spray-gun technique is practical for all work of this sort, whether paper cutouts or natural leaves are used. If three or four very thin coats are applied, there is little danger that paint or lacquer will seep under the edges of the cutouts or leaves.

Some time ago, the authors saw a most effective piece of modern wall decoration. It was, actually, India painting on a Weldwood panel measuring about 24 or 30 inches. It had been painted cream color and overlaid with an arrangement of oak, maple, and fern leaves. Then a jet-black paint had been applied and the leaves removed. The panel had been set into an authentic Victorian picture frame covered with white flat paint. The whole thing had cost little more than a dollar. Hung against a pastel-blue wall in the very modern room for which it was designed, it was not only a great credit to the young homemakers who planned and made it, but was also smart and appropriate in its setting. Nearby was a folding floor screen decorated in the same way.

New Fun with Old Stereoscopes

{ 6 }

Excitement ran high in Victorian families when Father brought home a new set of stereoscopic views of the Holy Land, Yellowstone Park, or Niagara Falls. Each member of the household eagerly awaited the moment when he was allowed to scan the scenic wonders of the world or to laugh heartily at the latest "comic." The stereoscope was itself one of the optical wonders of the world in 1870 (XXIV) when Grandpa was a boy.

The optical principle of the lifelike stereopticon was discovered many years ago by Sir Charles Wheatstone, an English scientist. Brushing aside the optical theory involved, we know that two pictures of the same scene or object, taken from very slightly different angles, mounted side by side and viewed through the simple optical machine invented by Wheatstone, give the illusion of a three-dimensional picture.

When these pictures are taken simultaneously with two cameras, the three-dimensional effect registers if the lenses of the cameras are about the same distance apart as human eyes. The stereoscopic cameras used in the 1870's (XXVI) were actually two cameras mounted in a single box. Their shutters operated together and exposures were simultaneous, side by side on the same photographic plate.

There are several simple ways to make stereoscopic views today. What is more, we may now take our own shots with a single Brownie, or similar type camera, although expensive stereoscopic cameras are for sale. Certainly there is no need for expensive equipment. You may also use two cameras (XXIII), in which case they are mounted on a board and the shutters operated together by means of a string. You must see to it, however, that the lenses are the required distance apart, as in XXVI, or the illusion will be destroyed. Dimensions given here are taken from old stereoscopic views, (XXV), and so will fit perfectly the old viewers.

You may get the same result by shifting a single camera to take two views one after the other. Anchor the camera by screwing it to a board which is mounted on a tripod. After one exposure, shift the camera to the opposite end of the board and make another. You should do this as quickly as possible to make sure that the light hasn't changed. If it is inconvenient to screw the camera down each time, slip a heavy rubber band over it and the baseboard.

Figure 19 shows a tripod board with small battens nailed to each end. As shown in 19, these act as stops for the camera. Obviously the size of the board will depend on the size of the camera. However, no matter what the camera's size, each picture must be taken with the critical between-the-eye distance corresponding to the distance between the centers of the stereoscopic views illustrated. Otherwise the effect will be diminished or lost completely.

If you don't want to go to the bother of making this mounting platform for your tripod, you may buy the inexpensive gadget shown with the two cameras, XXIII. It is attached to the tripod in the usual way and then the camera is attached to this; a sort of pantograph device, it is capable of shifting a measured distance. A picture is taken first at the extreme right, then the device is shifted and a second picture is taken with the camera at the extreme left.

You must keep track of your *right-* and *left-*hand pictures while developing, and be sure to develop them together in the same bath and for the same length of time. Printing calls for the same procedure. The negatives

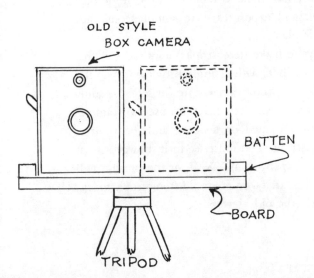

OLD STYLE BOX CAMERA

BATTEN

BOARD

TRIPOD

19. How a single box camera may be used to take scenes for stereoscopic viewing. First, a photograph is taken on one side of the board and then the camera is pushed to the other side of the board and the scene photographed again. When these exposures are mounted side by side on cardboard and then viewed through an old stereoscopic machine, there will be a three-dimensional effect.

XXIII. Stereoscopic views may be taken with two inexpensive cameras mounted side by side, with the shutters operated simultaneously by means of a string. Camera shops also carry the pantograph device shown with the cameras; with this, only a single camera is employed. First a photo is taken in one position and then the pantograph (which is attached to a tripod) is shifted in the opposite direction and the second picture is taken.

are placed side by side in the printing frame and exposed and developed together. You are looking for prints that are identical in every respect.

If you use very small cameras, you will need to enlarge the prints slightly to the size indicated in XXV. If this is necessary, the negatives should be placed in the enlarging camera together, exposed and developed together. Enlarging paper which offers the greatest possible contrast should be used. The greater the contrast in the prints, the greater the illusion of depth in viewing. This means using a fast, sensitive film—probably Super XX, developing it for maximum contrast and printing on paper such as 4F Azo. You then mount the prints on Bristol board just as they were photographed, *right* and *left*.

XXIV. An old-time stereoscopic viewer of the 1870's; this was the grand hobby of the amateur photographers. Millions of these were sold and are still available for very little in second-hand and antique shops.

XXV. If modern photographs intended for use with old stereoscopic viewers are to be successful, they must have these dimensions.

There is no need to purchase an expensive viewer. If the attic doesn't yield one, almost any antique or second-hand shop can turn one up for probably as little as a dollar. It will be just as serviceable as the day Grandpa bought it—and about the same price. There are still thousands of them around; several million were in use at one time.

While the photographs can be done in black and white, relatively in-expensive color film adds further incentive. A trip to Canada or to the Painted Desert still offers exciting entertainment as recorded for the stereoscope.

XXVI. A stereoscopic camera used by amateur and professional alike in the 1870's and 1880's.

Spray-Spatter for Today's Art

Spatter work as a craft was taken up in this country during Lincoln's Presidency and did not die out until the late 1880's. The process was simple and the results gratifying, and, consequently, the hobby was widely popular. Today few auctions of Victorian homesteads fail to yield one or more examples of this work done in the light of coal-oil lamps. Like most of the Victorian hobbies, it was often tenderly sentimental or of a religious nature.

Applied to paper, wood, or glass as well as to fabric, spatter was used for the decoration of many household articles: pictures for framing, monogrammed doilies and tidies of Swiss muslin, antimacassars, door panels, lampshades (XXVII), sofa pillows, chair seats, pincushions, table mats, and toilet sets. The motifs were supplied by combinations of cut paper and pressed leaves, stems, buds and flowers from plants and trees, grass, and seaweed.

The basic principle of spray-spatter can be illustrated by laying a piece of paper on a larger one of white and then spattering ink or water color over the whole surface. When the square of paper is removed, it leaves a plain square surrounded by spatter. The same is true if a fern, a flower, or a maple leaf is used; the possibilities are unlimited. Subtle variations for more complicated effects are desirable, including a nice control for shading, but all of them involve this first principle applied directly or in reverse.

Pleasing results in spray-spatter work come from arrangement even more than from the execution, which, with practice, is extremely simple. The woman who arranges flowers well but can't paint them will be delighted by what she can achieve with spray-spatter to preserve her arrangements indelibly. The careful worker spends a great deal of time arranging and rearranging the specimens on the piece to be spattered until a satisfactory combination is reached. The patterns illustrated here are from the late Victorian era; each one demonstrates the pleasing design that, with a little patience, can be achieved.

One of the simple problems of the craft can be easily solved if you take time out to make a botanist's press, illustration 10. Practically a must

XXVII. A segment of an attractive lampshade made in the 1870's by spattering ink on paper, cardboard, wood, or glass, to which ferns, leaves, or flowers have been pasted. After the spatter has been completed, the leaves or flowers are removed, leaving the outlines illustrated. (From Jones and Williams' *Making Household Elegancies*)

for the successful hobbyist in this field, it is easily constructed. The size of your press is determined by the size of the objects to be treated. Medium-sized fern leaves, for example, measure about twelve inches in length and almost four inches at the base of the fronds.

You will need two well-seasoned, absolutely warpfree pieces of hard-wood or plywood so that objects pressed between them will lie completely flat. If large boards are used for especially large leaves or flowers, it is necessary to install binding screws. They should be inserted at the center of the sides and ends, about one inch in from the edge. Ordinary stove bolts will do, with winged nuts for easy tightening with the fingers. These come in appropriate lengths. Place a washer on each bolt between the board and the winged nut to facilitate tightening for the maximum pressure. Specimens to be pressed should be left in the press for at least twenty-four hours. If a great many specimens are to be prepared, you will need more than one press. Drying as well as pressing will be considerably speeded up if the flowers or leaves are laid between two clean pieces of white blotting paper before they are placed between the boards of the press.

In setting up designs, straight pins, Moore pushpins, thumbtacks, or a bit of rubber cement will help. After you decide upon an arrangement, you must set it up so that it will create very sharp outlines when the spatter is applied. This means that each leaf, each stem, bud or monogram should lie as flat as possible on the surface to be spattered. In many instances, especially that of holding paper designs in place temporarily, rubber cement is excellent because it can be rubbed off easily after the spatter has been applied. Rubber cement is particularly helpful in cutting and placing a border of paper. See to it, however, that all traces of excess rubber cement are removed, because there will be no spatter covering those spots where it remains.

While it is quite true that many Victorian pieces were done with India or indelible ink, a wide range of colors was also used. The modern hobbyist may choose almost any color. Naturally, the paint—water-colors or colors mixed with alcohol—must be extremely fluid or it will not spatter well. When black is used, it should be very black; for this, there is no substitute for India ink, such as Higgins.

Ordinary water-colors are suitable for wall paper or pieces that are to be framed for use as spatter pictures, but, of course, are ruled out for patterns on washable fabrics, XXVIII. For these, Higgins waterproof inks come in a wide range of colors, as well as in black and white. Available at stationery and art-supplies stores, they are not expensive, and a single bottle will cover a large surface.

The Victorian hobbyist used to produce spray-spatter in one of two ways: by applying the ink either to a fine wire mesh or to the space between the teeth of a comb. In the case of the comb, the ink would spatter in tiny droplets when the fingers were run along the ends of the teeth.

XXVIII. Attractive spatterwork was done on fabrics using liquid dyes in place of ink. Some of this work was intricate and involved the ingenious use of several colors. (From Jones and Williams' *Making Household Elegancies*)

An easier and more effective method is to use a toothbrush, preferably one with stiff nylon bristles. If the brush is *moderately* filled with ink or water-color and a steel ruler is drawn across its bristles, they will snap back, shooting off the ink in a fine spray. But if excessive amounts of ink fill the brush, the result may be disastrous. Instead of a uniform, fine spray, relatively large drops of the ink or water-color will fall in ugly blots. Therefore, use caution, be patient, and always use an under- rather than an over-filled spatter device.

First, try for uniformity in covering the entire surface exposed in the panel you are working on, then shaded areas may be added. In the old days, it was the practice to increase the density of the spatter at the edges of the pattern, bleeding the ink off at the outer edge of the panel. There is a sound reason for this in that it sharpens the outline of the design by increasing and sharpening the contrast. As a technique, it is still effective.

Offhand, you might discount any possibility of flexibility in this craft, feeling that it is pretty much a matter of silhouetting natural motifs on white; but this is by no means the case. For one thing, black spatter against a white background may be reversed strikingly by the use of Higgins white ink against a black-paper background. Wonderfully decorative plaques and panels for the most contemporary décor can be made this way. Other color schemes can be worked out to fit a wide variety of room colors. By the use of colored Bristol board with Higgins colored inks, a wide range of combinations is possible; blue on gray, brown on yellow, pimento on

XXIX. Victorian ladies did spatterwork by filling the spaces between the teeth of a comb with ink and then running their fingers over the teeth to spray the ink on the work. A toothbrush with nylon bristles is much better for this purpose. A knife blade is used to flex the bristles in a direction opposite the work to be spattered, care being taken to test the spread of the spatter.

brown, yellow on green, shocking pink on dark green—these are a few of the many. Good color sense leads to endless satisfying effects.

Designs themselves may be rendered in color variations by a slight change in technique, one similar to those employed by the silhouettists of the early part of the nineteenth century. As an example, take a cross, XXIX, reversed. Say that we want to produce the cross in spatter rather than in a clean white silhouette. The cross is first drawn on a piece of paper large enough to cover the whole of the proposed panel. After the cross is cut out, the paper is placed over the panel and sprayed, leaving a spattered cross in whatever color chosen. The paper is then removed and the cross, already cut from the paper, is laid on top of the spattered image to cover it while the rest of the design is spattered in other colors. Contrasting colored borders may also be added in the same manner.

Innovations will occur to the imaginative worker as he proceeds. Originality and scope increase as you work out more forms. These may be used as shadows or in spattered areas or in a variety of motifs such as hearts, scrolls, cupids, crowns, crescents, skylines, anchors and ships, figureheads, birds in flight, etc.

Carefully executed in suitable colors and framed properly, these arrangements are just as appropriate in simple modern settings as they were to their elaborate Victorian background.

Pennsylvania Dutch Decor:
A Living Folk Art

{ 8 }

The industrious Pennsylvania Dutch have given us a rich heritage of folk art, for an important part of their culture lay in decorating everything they lived with. Their strongly superstitious natures were partly responsible, too, as evidenced by their barns, which were painted with colorful symbols to ward off the "evil spirits." They even decorated their household furniture and utensils. Every betrothed girl owned a gaily painted dower chest and a "bride's box," inscribed, as likely as not, with *"Ich liebe dich."* Even the family candle box did not escape their urge to mitigate the tedium and routine of the daily chores. As late as the 1840's, the country schools of Bucks County were still teaching children fractur which was applied with water colors to hymnals, wedding certificates, and sheets of music.

Some of these decorations were applied elegantly and with patience; some were careless and devoid of detail. But all had a charm that makes them treasured items for the collector of American antiquities. The continued popularity of this work has brought about a demand for rediscovering its techniques. Fortunately for those of us who have no real talent for painting, these are not difficult to master. Certainly not every German farmer, cabinetmaker, farm wife, daughter, or son who decorated household articles was an artist. Quite the contrary. A folk art that survives for centuries is established and carried on not by undiscovered Rembrandts but by average men and women.

While a relatively large number of Pennsylvania Dutch dower chests of the eighteenth and early nineteenth centuries are still about, most of them are in the hands of collectors or in museums. The few that reach antique dealers usually bear price tags that put them beyond the reach of the ordinary purchaser.

However, that shouldn't deter anyone who wants to own a reproduction. The plain unrefinished pine blanket chests made during the latter part of the eighteenth century or during the first half of the nineteenth are still plentiful in antique shops at prices ranging from $10 to $20. One can be made in the workshop at home for less than $10. All we need to convert an ordinary pine blanket chest into an acceptable specimen of a German dower chest are a few painted panels.

The old dower chests varied greatly in size. The largest were four feet long, two feet wide and two feet deep. The smaller chests were three feet long, and one-and-a-half feet wide and deep. Construction methods varied also—according to the maker. Pennsylvania Dutch farmers who could afford the services of a cabinetmaker owned chests with beautifully dovetailed corners, molding around the lid, scrolled bracket feet and, in rare cases, two well-fitted drawers at the bottom.

Farmers too poor to afford such finely executed pieces had to make their own. Through lack of skill and necessary tools, results at times were somewhat crude. These chests were not dovetailed at the corners; they lacked scrolled bracket feet and moldings cut by planes. Instead, the corners were nailed together as in any box. The molding around the lid was replaced by plain lathlike pieces that served to cover the crevice between the lid and the chest itself. They were sufficient to seal the chest against

20. Examples of Pennsylvania Dutch chest panels and the types of decorations and colors used in painting them.

moths and dust. The bracket feet were plain boards with no scrolling. Even the most amateur of home carpenters should be able to make that kind of a chest out of pine boards in a few hours.

Just as the craftsmanship in the construction of the dower chests varied, so did the painting. Sometimes a cabinetmaker painted the chest, sometimes a member of the family. Consequently, some chests showed natural talent, others a lack of artistry. In other words, German chests were in no way different from run-of-the-mill chests made throughout the country a century or more ago. Beautifully or plainly made, they were still authentic products of their period.

The decoration on all simple chests followed a general pattern. First there was a light panel with a suitable painted background, usually blue. Over this panel there was painted a jug or crock with flowers in it; sometimes tulips, sometimes flowers having no botanical counterpart. Colors were always gay and unrestrained.

The panels varied in size, number, and shape (20). Some had only two, some three and some five, with three on the front and one at each end. Here and there we find a chest with a lid design, but not in panel form. In rare cases the panels were painted with a maze of detail and with tulip, pink, or fuchsia designs worked in between them. Also, the names of the young couple and the date were inscribed.

Many designs were scratched in with a compass and a sharpened nail rather than with a pencil. Colors used most for panel decorations were bright blues, reds, greens, and yellows. Panel background colors ranged between off-white, cream, and buff, providing strong contrast for the flowers and leaves. Borders around the panels were often painted a shade of yellow. Before the panels were laid out and painted in, the chests were invariably painted a brilliant blue.

Illustration 20 shows not only the shapes of the various panels, but also supplies several drawings of authentic designs which can be enlarged and applied to chests by means of a stencil. This, however, is apt to produce a mechanical effect. If you feel up to it, draw in each of the panels, using a steel straight-edge, a sharpened nail, and a steel-pointed carpenter's compass to scratch in the outline. If you are not confident about tackling this process immediately, first draw in the design with a soft pencil and go over it with the instruments. It will give the decoration authenticity.

Before the blue over-all background is painted, put a sealer coat of thin shellac on the chest, especially if you are working with new pine or old pine that has been stripped and sanded. Follow the sealer coat with a single application of flat white; sand it lightly with oo sandpaper and dust before applying the blue.

Whatever the brilliancy of the original colors of the dower chest, the specimens that have come down to us have suffered from fading. It is safe to assume that the colors were quite flat when applied. However, the modern decorator, lacking the old paint mixtures, may choose between one of several mediums. He may use ordinary enamels (cutting the gloss with steel wool after they have set), he may mix his own oil colors, or he may use some of the almost limitless color possibilities offered by the pigments intended to be mixed with any of the water-thinned casein paints. This is an excellent paint, particularly when it has been covered with varnish and the surface given an antique glaze.

You may, of course, get any color combination by mixing colors ground

XXX. One of the more elaborately decorated Pennsylvania Dutch dower chests made during the latter part of the 18th century. (*Courtesy Metropolitan Museum of Art, New York*)

in oil and flat white paint with an oil base. Colors ground in oil are inexpensive and come in a wide range of shades. A small amount of color mixed with the flat white goes a long way. For instance, an inch of the pigment squirted from a tube colors a cupful of the white sufficiently. If you decide to use this material, start by adding small amounts of color to the flat white and build up to the value that you have in mind. If you reach a too-dark shade, you can always add more white.

If you use the extremely glossy, colored varnishes or enamels, you may tone them down either by rubbing with powdered pumice moistened with water (use a folded piece of felt for a rubbing pad), or by gently applying fine steel wool. The water-thinned casein paints, on the other hand, set with just about the right surface interest.

After the panels have been decorated with this paint, the whole chest is given one or two coats of dull varnish. If this is not available, use glossy varnish and cut down the shine with pumice or steel wool. In either

XXXI. A Pennsylvania Dutch bride's box made and painted during the early 19th century.

XXXII. More simple types of decoration on Pennsylvania Dutch dower chests from Bucks County. The smaller chests usually had two panels rather than three.

case, follow the rubbing-down by wiping the surface with a rag moistened with turpentine to pick up the remaining varnish and pumice dust.

"Antique glazing," as it is called, will give an antique effect to any painted surface. Starting with a cupful of a half-and-half mixture of Japan drier (supplied by paint stores in quarts or pints) and linseed oil in a soup plate, add some of the ground-in-oil colors mentioned previously. For this you will need a tube of raw umber, Van Dyke brown, and black. With a cupful of the drier-oil mixture, stir in about an inch of raw umber and the brown. To this add about ¼ inch of black as it is extruded from the tube. This combination when thoroughly mixed should give the right color.

Antiquing is quite easy. Work on only one panel of the chest at a time. Begin by painting over the panel (be sure that the panel has set for at least forty-eight hours after painting and before antiquing) with the mixture just prepared. When this is done, have a good supply of clean cotton batting on hand and a soup plate with an inch of clean turpentine in it. Use a wad of cotton about twice the size of a baseball, crush it in your hand, dip into the turpentine, and then wring it out until only moist. It may be necessary to wait for a few minutes until part of the remaining turpentine in the cotton has evaporated before the cotton is used—partly to wipe away and partly to shade the mixture that was painted over the panel which is still very wet.

Start by wiping the mixture away from the center of the painted panel. Remove less and less of the mixture back toward the border of the panel, shading and bleeding as you go along. You do not want streaks and, thus, you will have to replace the cotton wad with clean batting repeatedly—always moistened with turpentine. Very little of the antique glaze will need to be removed from the area near the border—just a very light brushing over and a smoothing out to uniform coloring will do.

Then the glazing mixture must set for a number of days before you give the chest its final coat of clear varnish. Otherwise, the varnish brush will pick up a part of the glazing mixture and redistribute it. You may use either dull or glossy varnish, for you will go over it with fine steel wool in any case. This gives the varnish surface the "tooth" needed to hold a good grade of furniture wax which, after it is buffed up by rubbing with a soft cloth, will give the glow so much admired by all "antiquers."

In addition to the chests, brides' boxes, and so forth, already mentioned, the Pennsylvania Dutch decorated all manner of wooden (and later cardboard) boxes, some called "Bible boxes," which were usually round or oval and made by coopers to resemble the old wooden peck measures but with covers. Among the motifs that predominated were doves, deer, parrots, pinks, tulips, and fuchsia. Bride boxes often had a not-too-angelic angel with wings stiffly attached, without benefit of perspective. Indeed, perspective of any sort is to be avoided—a fact that contributes greatly to the ease with which they may be imitated is that the Pennsylvania Dutch were two-dimensional artists. For a charming added effect you may want to inscribe *"Ich liebe dich"* on the bride's box you make—if you do, be sure to remember to use German lettering.

Decoration in the Pennsylvania Dutch manner can be fun and requires little skill. We assure the beginner that this art is as easy as we have tried to make it sound.

21. Catalog of motifs the Pennsylvania Dutch used in decorating furniture.

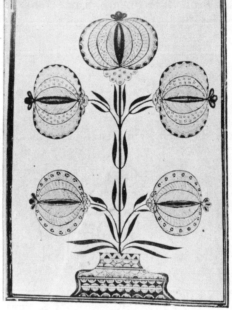

XXXIII. Specimens of fractur painting as done by Pennsylvania Dutch amateur artists during the early 19th century. Ink and water-colors were used in this manner to
decorate hymnals, sheet music, wedding certificates,
Bibles, etc., in this delightful folk art.

Berlin Wool Work for Needlecraft Novelties

{ 9 }

Walt Whitman was a struggling young poet, N. P. Willis was the most popular author in *Godey's Lady's Book,* and everyone was sitting for daguerreotypes when the craze for Berlin wool work struck America. Hoop-skirted ladies were quite aflutter. Yarn- and art-supply dealers alike were sorely pressed to meet the demand as every middle-class lady and her daughter began furiously to make ottoman, sofa, chair, slipper, and even pincushion coverings in the new fashion. For twenty years or more the craft flourished; it was finally laid low by the English Art School of Needlecraft which succumbed to the influence of Rossetti and his followers, Burne-Jones and Morris.

Not that Berlin wool work was new to the 1840's: it had its modest beginnings very early in the nineteenth century with an invention by an Englishman named Philipson. It was first sponsored, however, by the ladies of the Prussian capital, where Frau Wittich, wife of a print and book dealer, introduced it.

Dictionaries of the day called it "tapestry needlework." Actually, it was a substitute for embroidery which was declining in popularity and quality, although during the eighteenth century it had been the chief pastime of ladies of wealth, many of whom worked from designs by reputable artists. Louis XIV had hired a court embroiderer to copy the King's portrait after Lebrun, and the English Guild of Embroidery had been recognized as one of the Liveried Companies of London.

The craft of wool work, looked upon as a vulgarization of embroidery, however well it simulated it, had its inspiration in the latter part of the eighteenth century. Ladies outside the realm of state dinners and salon musicales began to mimic their more fortunate sisters by mounting cheap

73

XXXIV. An example of Berlin wool work done in America during the 1850's, when floral groups, scenes, and even portraits were wrought with yarn.

steel engravings on felt and working them in with colored yarns. Philipson merely set about making this popular form of embroidery simpler by printing colored designs on graph paper. Mounted on canvas, these required cross-stitching according to the pattern, in a perfectly mechanical manner. Women without the patience to master petit point responded in droves.

The first of these printed and hand-colored guidance sheets were simple geometric patterns and called for very little skill. As the popularity of the new craft grew, scenes, floral groups, and human forms were introduced.

By 1845, American devotees of Berlin wool work had an estimated 15,000 patterns from which to choose. Little sister no longer took her first lesson in needlecraft on a sampler. Her mother bought a simple Berlin (or English) pattern at the stationery store, thus ending a form of apprenticeship that had endured for almost two hundred years.

But in spite of the craft's popularity, few well-preserved specimens of American work have survived. Here and there one finds a scene or a floral group framed behind glass. Millions of moths have undoubtedly fattened on the rest of it, since it was probably done in wool of the merino sheep.

Nineteenth century women had three courses open to them: they could use Berlin patterns; old engravings stuck to canvas or linen and worked in with colored yarn; or, if they were very wealthy, they could employ an artist to make colored sketches directly upon the material. The modern woman also has several approaches to this work. She may purchase canvas or white linen already printed in outline or with transfers on paper, to be applied to fabrics with a warm iron. Or, she may express herself more independently by coloring and using old engravings. Again, she may make her own Berlin patterns on graph paper. Before going into details of this

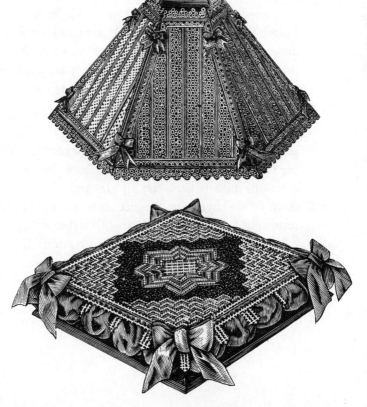

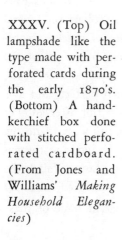

XXXV. (Top) Oil lampshade like the type made with perforated cards during the early 1870's. (Bottom) A handkerchief box done with stitched perforated cardboard. (From Jones and Williams' *Making Household Elegancies*)

technique, it might be of interest to read the comments of an old-time expert, Miss Emily Lambert, who published her *Handbook of Needlework* in 1842.

"Berlin patterns, although a production of recent date, have become an article of considerable commerce in Germany, where a large amount of capital is employed in their manufacture. They are either copied from celebrated pictures, or (as is more frequently the case) from the newest and most favourite engravings published either in England, France, or Germany. Many subjects, such as flowers and arabesques, are designed expressly. They are first drawn in colours on quadrille or point paper [cross-section, or graph, paper to be had at any stationery store]; and as the excellence of the pattern depends principally on the first design, it may readily be imagined that artists of considerable talent are required for their execution. From this drawing, an engraving or etching is made on a copper-plate, which has previously been ruled in squares of the required size, corresponding to the threads of the canvas: various marks and hieroglyphics are engraved on each check or square, which are to serve as guides for those who afterwards colour the impressions on paper; the part for each colour, or separate shade of colour, being marked with a different figure. The pattern, when in this state, bears a very great resemblance to those published in old books on needlework, above two centuries since; the present mode being, in fact, merely an improvement on the designs which have for years been used by weavers for their figured stuffs.

"The process of colouring these patterns is curious; the various tints are quickly laid on, commencing with each separate colour on several patterns at the same time, each check, or continuous line of checks, according to the engraved figures, being coloured by one stroke of the pencil, the point of which is kept very square, and of a size adapted to that of the check of the engraving. Practice alone renders the touch perfect; and it is surprising to see with what rapidity and exactness each tint after another is laid on. If we for a moment reflect on these different processes, and the time they must necessarily occupy, the expense of the design, and the engraving, and that each square is coloured by hand, we cannot fail to be surprised at the small cost at which they are to be procured; and our wonder will not be diminished when we are told, that in some of these patterns there are considerably above half a million of small squares like those of a mosaic, to be coloured.

"All Berlin patterns are equally adapted for working either in cross or tent stitch, although great judgment is requisite in choosing them. Patterns intended to be enlarged by the working, should be closely shaded, or the colouring, being dispersed, will appear meagre. Difficulties frequently arise from working these designs without previously fixing on the colour of the background. This should always be done in the first instance, as a pattern, to work well, must always be shaded, or sorted, with strict attention to the colour of the ground; a maxim which is but too frequently neglected. Most of the figure patterns may, with a fair knowledge of painting, and a just idea of light and shade, be much improved, as many of them are extremely correct in the outlines, although the colouring of most is harsh and glaring in the extreme—a defect which it is the province of the expert needlewoman to overcome. In this respect, however, there is frequently a great difference even in the colouring of the same design. In sorting the wools for working historical subjects, attention to a few of common rules of painting will be found useful in correcting some of the more gross of these errors, such as, for instance, the back and foreground being of the same depth of shade. Black should never be used next to a high light; one-eighth of every object has a high light upon it, one-eighth is darkest shadow, and six parts light and half tint. No objects in nature are *positively* blue, red, or yellow, owing to two causes: one, that most objects reflect the sky; the other, that the atmosphere between the eye of the observer and the object causes the brightness of the tints to be deadened. It hence arises that care must be taken to avoid the immediate contact of bright colours with each other, where any attempt is made to imitate nature the *contrary* of which, it would appear, was the point to be arrived at in some of the Berlin patterns.

"In some patterns, when harmony of colour alone is to be sought, it is easier to avoid these defects; but a few of the more necessary rules to be observed, independent of the guidance of taste, may not be unacceptable. Scarlets and yellows assort very ill, and browns and lilacs are also lost upon a scarlet ground; blues and greens are bad together, as well as yellow and green. On the contrary, almost all the class of drabs and fawns (called by the French *écrus,* and used by them with such exquisite taste), are good

XXXVI. A shallow shadow box with a built-up laminated cross cut from perforated cardboard (unstitched) and decorated with small dried flowers. (From the authors' collection)

XXXVII. Crosses done with laminations of cardboard were very popular during the 1870's. Here is a suggested design from an art catalog of that time. The lacy border was done with the same material.

with blue; the colder and greener shades with lilacs; the deep rich brown-toned drabs are beautiful with yellow; pinks and greys are good; scarlets and slates; greens and red browns; greens and maize, with some shades of salmon colour; blue with maize; lilac with green; and blue with claret; all will be found generally to please the eye.

"The greatest difficulty which we have to encounter in selecting the colours for figure patterns, is the face; so many totally different colours and shades are here required to produce, when worked, what should appear to be almost as one, and here the skill of the needlewoman will be fairly put to the trial. The skies and clouds are also difficult to manage; the greatest nicety being required in the blending of the various colours, and to avoid the *liney* appearance which will but too frequently appear.

"Berlin patterns can be copied on cloth, satin, or other materials by stretching a canvas over them, and working through the threads, which are afterwards to be drawn out. On cloth, however, it is better not entirely to withdraw the threads, but only to cut them off close to the work; by this means, when mounted, it will have a much richer and closer appearance, and if intended for articles of furniture, will wear much better. In groups of flowers, the small interstices of ground which sometimes appear between the leaves, are better worked with a wool exactly corresponding to the colour of the cloth than to cut out the threads, an uniform surface being thus given to the whole work.

"For working these patterns on Berlin, or silk canvas, the same rules are applicable as for canvas intended to be grounded; but it may not be improper to remark, in this place, on a method of mounting small pieces of work on Berlin canvas, which has been copied from the Germans, namely, that of placing a painted sky behind the canvas. Good needlework requires no foreign aid for its display; but here, on the contrary, instead of receiving any such, a mean and paltry appearance is frequently given to it. Vignette and flower pieces, even when worked on white silk canvas, may sometimes be appropriately lined with coloured satins or velvets, to take away from the otherwise cold appearance of the ground; but the lining should always be of one uniform colour. Coloured silk canvas should be lined with a coloured ground in accordance with their several tints."

Like the copycat ladies of the eighteenth century, however, we may color an old steel engraving, mount it on canvas, and work in the color in simple cross-stitch, or we may bravely set about blocking out our own or copied designs on graph paper, which is supplied in sheets of various size and with ruled-off sections of sizes up to ¼ inch. Chromatic guidance is supplied with water-colors, and we need not start to fill in with yarn until we are satisfied with the paper preparation.

As for old steel engravings, second-hand bookstores can supply them literally by the ton, many of them to be found for twenty-five cents each.

After Berlin wool work had become just a memory, a closely related form of needlecraft suddenly blossomed forth during the 1860's. If Berlin wool work was a vulgarization of embroidery, the new craze was a vulgarization of wool work. Like the ladies of the earlier nineteenth century who had been scandalized by Philipson's printed cards, the ladies of the mid-1860's were shocked by the appearance of the perforated cards offered as guides to stitching. This was the new and final decadence, beneath the dignity of ladies of leisure and social standing. While Berlin wool work had attracted one recruit, perforated card work attracted twenty—or fifty!

This came about because an American mechanical genius developed a machine capable of perforating cardboard with small round holes, holes just small enough for a silk thread to pass through or just large enough for yarn. Now it was possible not only to print designs to guide the needle

but to supply holes through which the needle could be plied without effort. Surely only *hoi polloi* could accept such a pastime.

And how the *hoi polloi* accepted it! One of the most popular forms of the new craft was the Biblical quotation "Remember Me," with a cross which was hung over the head of the bed. Another was a tenderly expressed sentiment sometimes done on small cards with human hair. We have in our collection of this work one very small strip of perforated paper glued to blue ribbon with the inscription, "Dear Mary's Hair." In earlier days, it was not unusual for families to keep notebooks with braided hair of deceased members sewn to the pages with appropriate sentiments written beneath them. Some types of the perforated card, framed in black walnut behind glass, are still abundant, bringing as little as fifty cents in hinterland auctions.

These perforated cards came in all sizes, both printed and plain, and the work was not limited to the framed quotation. A wide variety of ornamented "elegancies" were so decorated—cardcases, handkerchief boxes, bookmarks, wall baskets, lampshades, duster pockets. Here, too, advice

XXXVIII. Few were the middle-class young ladies of the 1870's who did not try their hand at stitching mottoes in perforated cardboard. Such board was sold in most stationery stores with printed guidance for the stitching. The left specimen, "No Cross, No Crown" was done by the mother of one of the authors.

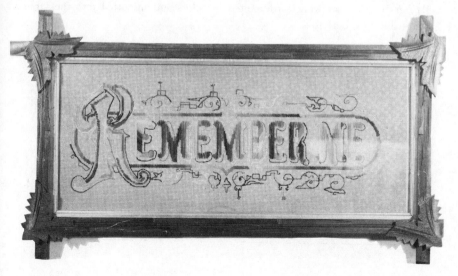

XXXIX. Perforated cardboard with holes of various sizes was supplied, some large enough to accommodate 4-ply yarn, others delicate enough to pass only fine silk. Here was a sort of sampler done by a young lady of the 1870's. (From the authors' collection)

was often found in mottoes: "Press Forward to the Mark of Your High Calling," "Be Diligent in Well Doing," or "Remember the Sabbath Day to Keep it Holy."

The cards made any straight-line geometric pattern easily possible with no strain on the eyes, the purse, or artistry. Hence, the prodigious production which represented the last stage in a long-drawn-out deterioration of

XL. A Berlin wool work card printed in colors and imported into the United States during the 1840's.

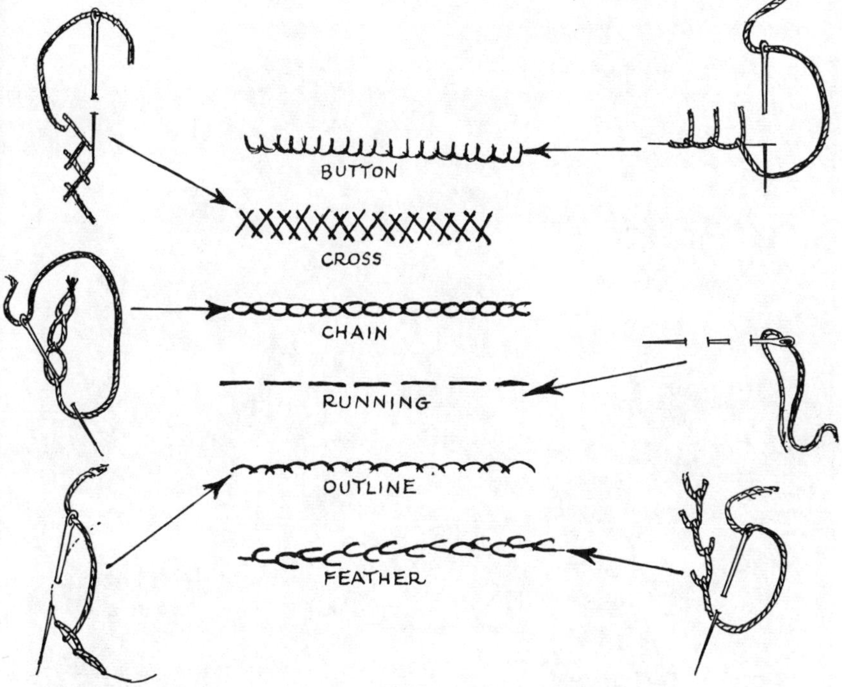

BUTTON

CROSS

CHAIN

RUNNING

OUTLINE

FEATHER

22. The simplified basic embroidery stitches such as those used to make the articles described in this chapter.

needlecraft. Those who worked with the perforated card had the choice of using either yarn or other kind of thread. Some of the smaller and more ably executed samples in our collection are done with silk on cards with extremely small perforations. One piece, a distinct deviation, is done with white yarn on a piece of board that had been dyed black. The craft did offer some latitude for originality, meager as it was. Most existing samples of the work, however, are done in brightly colored yarn. Occasionally one finds an unframed specimen embellished with shells, silver, gold, or steel beads.

Working the stitched cards into lampshades, boxes, or cardcases was made very easy by binding the edges of the units with gay ribbon which in turn could be sewn to the binding on other pieces. Boxes were lined with silk or velvet. To render such articles more acceptable to the Victorian ladies of the day, some well-stocked stationery stores offered perforated paper in gold and silver. The insides of lampshades were often covered with green or red tissue paper which showed through the perforations.

XLI. Mary Ann Markey worked this sampler in homespun linen in 1820, when she was 12 years old. For over 200 years the young women of America took their first lessons in stitchery in this fashion. (*Courtesy Essex Institute, Salem, Massachusetts*)

But we should not be disparaging about this work. It still offers interesting possibilities in new and more original forms. With modern frames, the pieces might add an interesting note to many rooms.

When we reviewed the literature on this subject, the technique appeared simple enough. The hitch came when we attempted to find the perforated cardboard needed. We were assured that such material was available, but not at local stores. Big-city craft workers who itch to take a fling at the craft may be more successful. However, not to be denied at least a try at this business, we used a substitute.

This was made by pasting ordinary graph paper on cardboard thin enough to be punctured easily by a large or small needle. If you use heavy, colored yarn to work in a design, ⅛-inch-square graph paper should be just right. If you use silk thread, any paper with the smallest squares will be suitable. Guided by these lines and aided by a ruler and a soft pencil, you will find it easy to letter the paper. The letters indicated in pencil are then outlined with colored yarn. Simple running stitches may be ⅛ inch to 2 inches in length. The yarn should not be pulled too tightly or the cardboard may warp.

We found it expedient first to draw the design or the motto in fine lines with colored crayon. If red yarn were to be used, a red crayon was chosen. To approximate the quaintness of old examples, bright blues, reds, yellows, and greens should be selected.

Wool work is set off to advantage by a border and is given authenticity by being mounted in a late-Victorian walnut frame.

XLII. Stitching an old engraving with yarn, a hobby originated by middle-class German women during the 1780's.

The stitches made with 4-ply colored yarn through the plastic screening are guided with a piece of cross-section paper on which the motto to be worked has been drawn and filled in with colored crayons. A piece of this paper in the process of preparation is shown in XLIII.

When completed, the colored sketch of the letters is glued to the back of the plastic screening, which is in turn held tightly to a wooden frame by tacks. When the work is finished, the remaining paper is torn away and the screening with its worked-in motto is sewn to a piece of white silk or other cloth and made ready for framing.

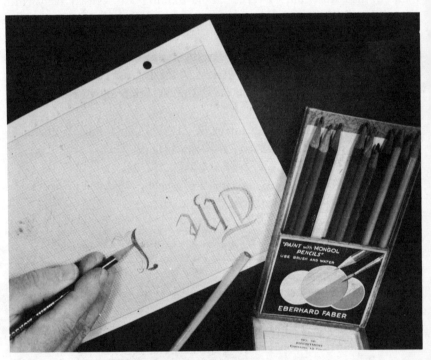

XLIII. Preparing cross-section paper with design and lettering done with colored pencils. The prepared design is thereafter glued to duck or other material and worked in with colored yarn.

The Look of Distinction: Hand-Printed Fabrics

{ 10 }

The 1656 inventory of the convicted New England "witch," Anne Hibbins, itemized "5 Painted Callico curtains and valients"—an enviable possession that might well have been a factor in her indictment. Such luxuries reached the colonial market through a long and tortuous route: from the Orient to Europe, through the East India Trading Company, and thence to the few citizens of New England who could afford to buy them. They were the *toiles peintes* of the day, and it was not until post-Revolutionary times that they became generally fashionable and within the reach of all but the poor provincials of the hinterlands.

Excitement ran high at Clifford's Wharf in Philadelphia during the late 1780's when a British ship arrived with a partial cargo of the latest styles in hand-printed calicoes, muslins, and chintzes to delight the hearts of the American women who could afford them. But a few years earlier the enraged women of the colonies had burned their gowns because the fabrics had been woven in England and printed for export by such firms as Peel and Yates. Among all the bitter protests from a tax-bedeviled people, this was perhaps the most astonishing. When a lady willfully destroys her most cherished finery she is very angry indeed!

It was a combination of anger, envy, and cost that sponsored the American craft—long since expired—of home-printing calico and other fabrics. Though technical advances in textile manufacture put an end to a widespread practice of the craft, it has definite appeal today for women in search of self-expression which promises individuality both in dress and in home decoration. Hand-printing fabrics offers a satisfaction vastly greater than the time it takes to master it.

Calicoes were hand-printed commercially in this country at a very early date. In 1715 one Francis Dwing advertised in a Boston newspaper that he "cuts neatly in wood and printeth calicoes." A few of the other craftsmen worked in the medium cut printing blocks of maple, pearwood, or holly to sell to ambitious women who not only did their own printing but lent their treasured blocks to friends and relatives so that they might share the high fashion of the day. Though most samples of old-time block printing are on calico, and a few on linen and muslin, many kinds of cotton fabrics are equally suitable.

There is hardly a book dealing with home crafts that does not devote some space to printing on paper with designs cut from linoleum. Substituting dye for ink and wood for linoleum, we have the requisites for block-printing fabrics. And, there is no reason why the more easily cut linoleum cannot be used, so long as it is tacked to a solid block of maple about $1\frac{1}{2}$ inches thick. The wood itself must be strong enough to withstand repeated blows from a mallet.

Inexpensive woodcarving hand tools, now supplied in sets, are adequate for making wooden printing blocks and for linoleum as well. In any event, deep intricate carving is not necessary if the beginner can overcome the urge to indulge in complicated designs. The carving need only be deep enough (say $\frac{1}{8}$ inch) to insure a sharp outline.

In large measure, the difference between a good carver and a poor one is that the good carver has learned that clean, fast carving cannot be done with the equivalent of a ten-cent-store paring knife. Woodcarving good enough for block printing can be done with a top-quality jackknife if it is constantly honed. By constantly we mean that in carving a relatively simple block in maple, it may be necessary to touch up the blade as many as 50 or 60 times.

While women may protest the suggestion that they carve their own printing blocks from wood, the operation actually is not difficult. The block of wood must be thoroughly seasoned and must be perfectly flat. Our ancestors often used maple or applewood. Maple is semi-hard and close-grained—and possibly difficult for a woman to carve. There is no reason why soft white pine cannot be used instead; this can be cut with great ease. The problems of the beginner in woodcarving are greatly reduced if he pauses frequently to reestablish the cutting edge of his tiny chisels. A fine grit carborundum stone should be kept handy and used after each few

XLIV. Cutting a wooden printing block with small wood-carving chisels.

cuts. Close-grain and across-grain cutting cannot be clean unless tool edges are kept razor-sharp.

The design is first drawn on paper with a very soft pencil making heavy lines. This drawing is laid face-down on the clean block of wood and transferred by being rubbed firmly either with the side of a pencil or with a blunt, hard object. This leaves the penciled outline on the block which should again be traced with a sharp pencil to make the outline incisive. Then start cutting with a sloyd carving knife, safer than a jackknife, or—better still—a set of small carving chisels similar to those illustrated in XLIV. X-acto has a handy kit for this purpose. Begin by scoring deeply the outline of the design with the point of a very sharp knife. The outline should be retraced several times with the knife, using heavy pressure, so that a cut about ⅛ of an inch deep is made. Then, simply remove the wood outside of the design to a depth of about ⅛ of an inch. Thus, a printing surface is left raised by this distance above the surface of the block.

In most cases, the flat chisel of the carving set suffices to remove the surplus wood. As the cuts near the deeply-scored design are made, there should be perfect separation at these points. The sub-surface or non-printing surface does not need to be smooth. For the small circles in the centers of the flowers in the design, the cutting edge of the chisel is too large. Use, instead, the point of an ordinary knife to chip out the wood.

In the earlier days of fabric-printing at home, there was small choice of coloring matter. Indeed, housewives dyed their own yarn with home-brewed concoctions of boiled sumac or oak nut-galls with copper as a mordant. The more fortunate dames in the hinterlands bought indigo, madder, and cochineal from the peddlers. A book published in Boston in 1830, *The Frugal Housewife* by Mrs. Child, provides many of the old formulas. Light colors were to be steeped in brass and dark ones in iron. Yellow came from saffron or peach leaves, and black from rusty nails and vinegar. To "strike" a color meant to "set" it.

The modern hobbyist, of course, need not resort to such unscientific methods. The corner drugstore offers all the ingredients needed, including packaged dye powders in a multitude of shades.

By a simple procedure, ordinary powdered dye is readily usable. While such dyes may be made up in quantity sufficient to submerge a dress, the block printer needs a much smaller amount and in more concentrated form. He simply uses less water. The actual amount needed depends upon how much surface is to be covered and how much solid color is to be carried to the fabric by the block. In most cases, no more than half a cup of dye is needed. To give the dye necessary "body," add enough gum arabic to the hot mixture to give it the approximate consistency of cream. See that the gum arabic is thoroughly dissolved and very smooth with no lumps.

After cooling, the dye is applied to a soft piece of folded cotton, five or six folds of which are tacked over a plain wooden block. Press the printing block evenly into the wet cotton, thereby transferring the dye to the printing block. Extreme care must be taken to lay the printing block face-down on the fabric to be printed so that you will not smear the outline by any sidewise movement. Once in the proper position, hold and press the block firmly on the fabric and strike it sharply with a small wooden mallet to make a clean impression. The same care must be taken in removing the block. A slight twist will cause a smudgy outline. The small amount of gum arabic in the printed material will wash out easily.

A more expert formula for a suitable dye-ink involves adding ½ ounce of gum tragacanth to a cup of water and letting this stand for twenty-four hours, after which the mixture is stirred with an egg beater. After it has stood for a second twenty-four hours, again stir vigorously and add five to eight drops of carbolic acid. Then add a small amount of the dye to be used to boiling water and add that to the gum water; it is then ready to use.

Many people experienced in printing fabrics by hand find that du Pont Pontamine dyes are by far the best for this purpose. A typical formula for such printing is as follows:

Three grams of Pontamine dyestuff are added to ¼ cup of boiling water. This is added to the gum-tragacanth-water mixture above, along with three grams of sodium phosphate.

Rather than resort to the old-fashioned method of printing fabrics, the impatient modern hobbyist may wish to use one of the new, specially prepared colorings—available from such sources as Carter's Bray-Art, Fabricolor, and the American Crayon Company's Prang Textile Colors. Prang Colors come in twenty-two shades, are inexpensive and easily applied, and once applied they resist fading by washing, dry cleaning, and sunlight. They may be used for wood or linoleum block printing.

For mixing Prang Colors use a clean piece of glass and add Prang Extendor No. 1196 and Prang Hand Block Printing Extendor No. 1199. Mix with a spatula until the color is uniform. The color is applied to the wooden printing block by means of a rubber roller of the type sold in a photographic supply store. Run the roller back and forth over the colors on the glass and then over the surface of the printing block. Then carefully lay the block on the fabric to be printed and strike with a mallet as described above.

Allow the work to dry for twenty-four hours and then "set" it with heat. Cover the right side of the work with a clean, dry cloth and iron over that cloth with an electric iron heated to about 350°F., as you would in ordinary ironing, about three minutes; then repeat on the opposite side. Using a damp cloth as you would in pressing woolens, repeat the entire operation and you have fast colors.

XLV. A beautiful example of block printing from the latter part of the 18th century, done in blue by Elizabeth Pierce Throop of Rehoboth, Massachusetts.

As in other hobbies of the period, there were variations on block print-ing, some of which were used not only for printing fabrics but also for stamping patterns to be used as outlines of design for embroidering.

Some of the printing blocks used in the eighteenth century had surfaces made of metal strips embedded in soft wood. They were used by profes-sional craftsmen during the late 1790's and the first twenty years of the nineteenth century; Victorian ladies were offered manufactured kits for printing as late as the 1860's. These kits included twenty printing blocks, powdered dyes in various colors, a brush, dye-pad, and bottle of gum arabic.

While it may be surmised that these kits were intended primarily for the home stamping of embroidery designs, the supply of dyes of different colors leads to the assumption that other printing was also intended. More difficult to understand is the need for such kits at a time when printed materials were widely and inexpensively distributed; factories were print-ing materials from engraved copper rolls, a commercial development intro-duced during the early part of the nineteenth century. Evidently many Victorian ladies wanted to while away their idle hours in the pursuit of home crafts not dictated by economy.

We include a description of such block printing only with the thought that here and there may be found a husband-wife combination of con-firmed hobbyists who still may want to take a fling at this sort of work. If the husband, in particular, is handy with tools, he may find it easier to make such blocks than the hand-carved sort.

We have in our extensive collection of things relating to early crafts a number of the wood blocks with printing surfaces either of tin (early) or of brass (later). These blocks were soft and often cut from applewood. Long strips of tin or brass bent to conform with the design selected were driven edgewise into the blocks of wood *with* the grain. Working across the grain would have been far more difficult. The end of a raw block of wood about two inches thick, into which the metal strip was to be driven, was sanded down enough to make tracing the design with a soft pencil a bit easier. This traced design was used as a guide or pattern for bending the metal strip with the aid of pliers.

When the strip was formed, the worker proceeded to drive the strip into the wood edgewise, hammering the metal in at one end just far enough

XLVI. Commercial home-printing blocks made with brass strip imbedded in the end grain of applewood; from a kit supplied to mid-Victorian housewives.

to anchor it. Then a maple block large enough to cover the whole design was placed over the top edge of the strip and struck heavily and repeatedly with a hammer until about one-half on the half-inch strip was driven into the wood. Doing this assured the top edge of the strip's being level; if one part of the design so outlined were higher than another, printing would be difficult.

While tin strips were used for printing blocks in the early days, the kits supplied to Victorian fancyworkers contained rolled brass strips. Those who want to try their hand at this will find rolled brass at large hardware stores. The brass should be graded as soft and about 20-gauge.

Some of the early users of printing blocks were also able to achieve the solid effects of carved wooden blocks by packing felt flock into the open spaces of the design. The effect may have been imperfect as far as distribution of dye was concerned, but most impressions made with any

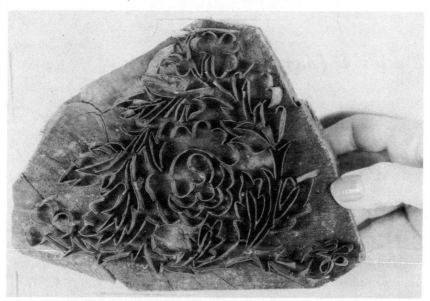

XLVII. Old-time printing block made by hammering tin strips into the end grain of applewood blocks. Such crude printing surfaces were used extensively during the 1820's.

form of block require touching-up with a brush here and there. This needn't be a cause for concern when dealing with small pieces. The touching-up is done with a brush dipped into a more liquid solution of the dye.

Home-printed fabrics offer many possibilities for highly individual home decoration. Curtains, tablecloths, table mats and napkins, spreads, wall hangings, and many other items suggest themselves. Obviously, one does not need to hold to the old motifs and designs, charming as many of them were.

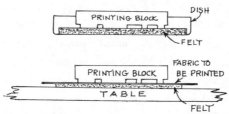

23. (Top) Felt or other fabric ink- or dye-pad placed in a shallow tin dish. (Bottom) The fabric to be printed is separated from the table by a piece of felt or several layers of cotton. Otherwise, irregular impressions will result.

Beauty & Color in Tinware

{ 11 }

How well those shrewd Yankee peddlers knew how to catch the fancy of their hinterland customers! While printed calicoes were first in popularity, hand-painted and stenciled tinware was not far behind. Few carts left New England without an array of gaily painted sconces, bread trays, canisters, and sugar bowls. During the early part of the nineteenth century, Connecticut, and particularly the town of Berlin, produced millions of pieces of the charming ware now so zealously sought by collectors—and at high prices. Most of the New England ware was stenciled, but the tinware of Pennsylvania showed that hand-painted decoration was also in vogue. Both forms of decoration involve techniques so simple that they may be mastered easily by those of us with little special talent. We have a rich selection of old designs to draw from. The modern tinker can easily make almost exact duplicates of the early ware, using as his raw material the lowly tin can. All the tools he needs are a small pair of tinner's snips, a hammer, a mallet, a 75-watt soldering iron, and a bit of solder, as well as a basic apprenticeship in tinkering.

Here and there among the antique shops and second-hand stores you will find old tin pieces suitable for decorating: trays, candlesticks, candle boxes, sconces. Some are plain, some bear the last vestige of a design that once delighted an early nineteenth-century grandmother. Rarely, however, do you find articles with well-preserved decoration that are inexpensive. In most cases old paint on tinware must be removed with modern solvents, scrubbed carefully, and then treated vigorously with fine steel wool.

Those who are unable to discover enough old tinware to decorate in the quaint old manner should not despair. There are many tin cans about, and fabrication with the simple equipment suggested is easy. In some cases,

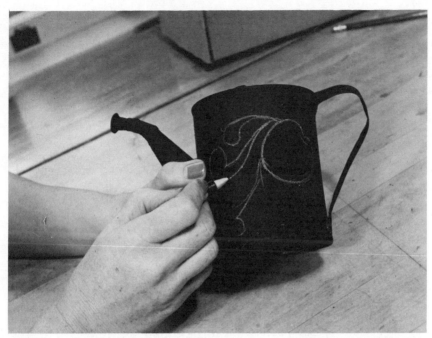

XLVIII. Amateur artists who have not yet mastered the brush strokes illustrated in 27 may wish first to draw designs with a soapstone or wax pencil.

XLIX. Authentic old tinware decorated with the "love apple" (tomato) and brush strokes. (*Courtesy New England Society for the Preservation of Antiquities*)

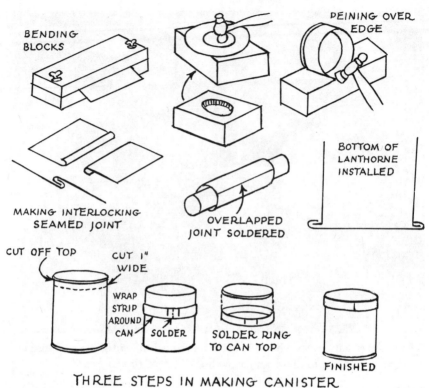

BENDING BLOCKS

PEINING OVER EDGE

MAKING INTERLOCKING SEAMED JOINT

OVERLAPPED JOINT SOLDERED

BOTTOM OF LANTHORNE INSTALLED

CUT OFF TOP

CUT 1" WIDE

WRAP STRIP AROUND CAN

SOLDER

SOLDER RING TO CAN TOP

FINISHED

THREE STEPS IN MAKING CANISTER

24. Simple procedures in bending, forming, fabricating, and tinware joints.

25. Tinware articles can be easily fabricated from tin cans of various sizes.

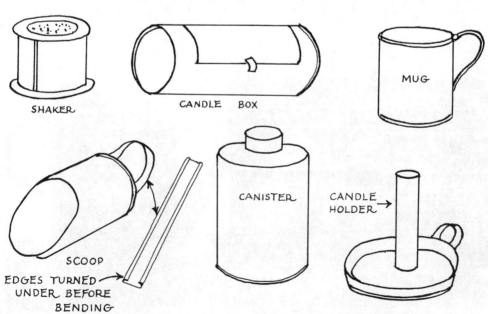

SHAKER

CANDLE BOX

MUG

SCOOP

EDGES TURNED UNDER BEFORE BENDING

CANISTER

CANDLE HOLDER →

a few cuts and a bit of bending and soldering will convert a can quickly into a perfect duplicate of ware made during the 1820's when the craft reached its peak of popularity.

First, a few pointers for working with sheet tin—really not tin at all, but sheet iron covered with a very thin layer of tin to protect it against rust. In the old days hot sheets of iron were dipped in molten tin. Today the tin is deposited by electrolysis for a very thin coating. Tin-plate is, then, a form of sheet iron, agreeably malleable and therefore shaped easily with a ball peen hammer. Ordinarily, however, to form tin-plate—as in bending at right angles—you can use a wooden mallet. It is relatively soft and so is dented easily by a steel hammer which leaves unsightly dimples and dents. Tinsmiths bend tin-plate in a machine known as a brake. If you want a clean, sharp bend, you will have to use two hardwood blocks, as in 24, and a mallet rather than a hammer. Say, for instance, you are making the tube needed for a candlestick. To obtain a sheet of tin-plate of the necessary size, merely cut the top and bottom off of a large tomato-juice can and slit the remaining cylinder, cutting away the joint. Then bend that piece of metal around a wooden mandrel held in a vise. The mandrel may be a maple dowel obtainable at any lumber yard. Simply solder the overlapping joint, as in 24, according to directions that will follow.

Some articles, such as sugar scoops, are easily converted from an ordinary soup can. You need cut only part of the can away (25) and add a handle by soldering. To strengthen the handles—they were used on many pieces of old ware—and to remove raw edges, you must take a strip of metal and turn the edges over as shown in the photograph. Put the strip of metal between the hardwood blocks and bend the edges about ⅛ inch over to a 90-degree angle with a mallet. Then remove the metal from the press and hammer it down to form the beaded edge.

If you want to hollow out a piece of tin-plate, work with a ball peen hammer and a dishlike depression in a hardwood block as shown in 24. The secret of success here is many light blows, rather than a few heavy ones, because they produce a minimum of surface defects.

The method used in producing such articles as cookie tins, salt shakers, and other small objects is illustrated in 24. Cookie tins require the large-size juice cans cut down to a height of seven inches. For one unused to tinner's snips, this cutting-down is not as easy as it may sound, and a fine-toothed hacksaw may be found more satisfactory. You can smooth off the raw edge with a fine file. Sawing is facilitated by putting the can over a large wooden mandrel held in a vise and sawing one inch at a time.

Rims of the covers of containers must be of slightly greater diameter than the bases if they are to fit. Making the cover is easy: first, using the snips, trim off the metal left on the can top. Next, bend a strip of tin about an inch wide around the cut bottom half of the can. This strip can be taken from the excess metal previously cut away, but it will be obvious that this isn't quite enough. The problem is solved as shown in 24. The joint is soldered while the metal strip is in place around the bottom half of the can. This is the only way to guarantee a proper, tight fit.

The resulting metal ring is now slipped off the bottom half of the can, which was used as a soldering guide. This ring is then soldered to the can top; it will be of about the same diameter as the outer edge of the top. Soldering is done on the *inside* to avoid a messy appearance. The container is then ready for washing in warm soapy water to remove all traces of grease and fingerprints before the ground coat of paint is applied. See to it that any soldering flux that may have seeped through the joint during soldering is carefully removed, for paint will not hold to it.

The soldering kit needed for this work is not only inexpensive, but its use is easily earned. A 75-watt electric soldering iron is first on the list. Add a few feet of solid wire solder and a small can of good grade of soldering paste or flux. A little preliminary practice on some odd piece of tin will soon give you the experience and confidence you need to assemble a variety of things from large juice cans. Tin cans are easiest to solder because tin is the chief ingredient of solder. There is, therefore, a natural affinity between the tin in the can and the solder.

The first rule of good soldering is a clean surface. If the surface to be soldered is suspect, make sure that it is clean, brushing it over gently with

26. A simple stenciled eagle decoration from an old tray done in solid gold or bronze. This was a favorite motif during the late Federal Period, 1815-1825.

27. Brush strokes commonly used to decorate tinware in the olden days.

the finest grade of steel wool before applying the flux or soldering paste.

Contrary to amateur notions about soldering, the deposit of a large amount of solder does not assure a strong joint. Rather, it is applied sparingly with *plenty of heat* so that the solder will flow out into a smooth, thin film.

Apply heat by holding the tip of the soldering iron to the spot to be soldered *after* the soldering flux or paste has been applied, or, if you wish, you may heat the spot and then apply the flux. At any rate, the surface, as well as the soldering iron must be heated enough to melt the solder. If the surface is heated far below the melting point of the solder, the solder will form in small globules and refuse to flow and to adhere to the tin surface.

Now, assume that a small handle is being soldered to a tin cup. The first operation is tinning each surface to be joined—that is, covering the

L. Trimming a fruit-juice can with a hack saw.

LI. Bending a piece of tin-plate between two pieces of hardwood to insure a sharp, clean angle.

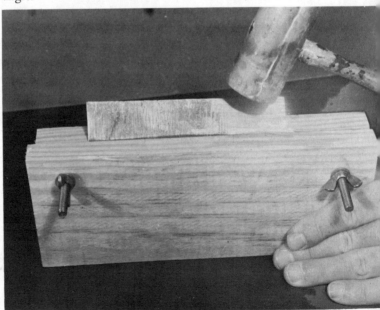

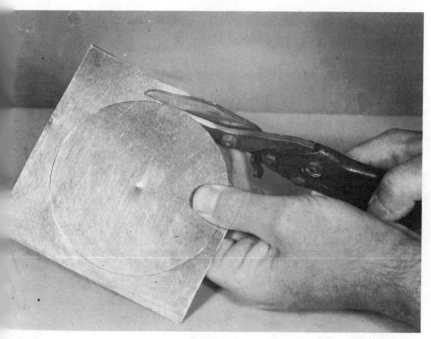

LII. Cutting out a disc which is to form the bottom piece of a home-fabricated tin lantern.

LIII. Peening over the edge of the tin disc to form the bottom joint as illustrated in 24.

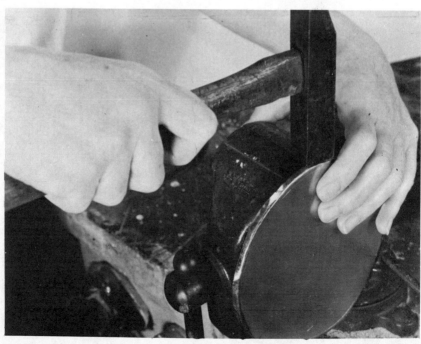

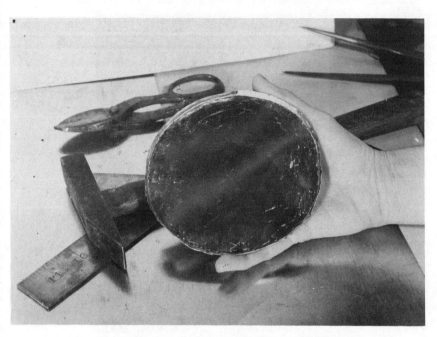

LIV. Finished bottom piece with the edge turned up.

LV. Peening over the bottom edge of a tin cylinder for the installation of a bottom piece as shown in **LVI** and **LVII**.

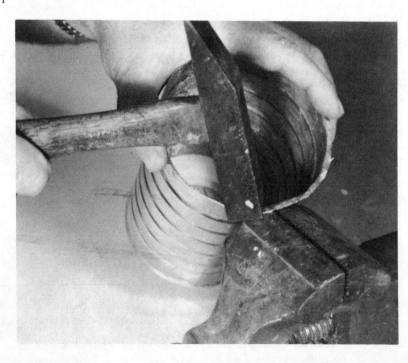

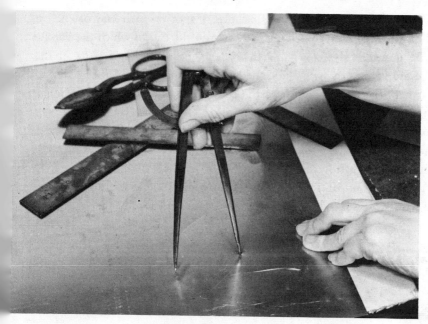

LVI. Tools needed for laying out tin-plate for cutting and for making designs in preparation for perforating.

LVII. Using a chisel to produce a perforated design in tin-plate. If a tin can is placed over a soft wood mandrel held in a vise, such designs may be worked in even though the tin does not lie flat.

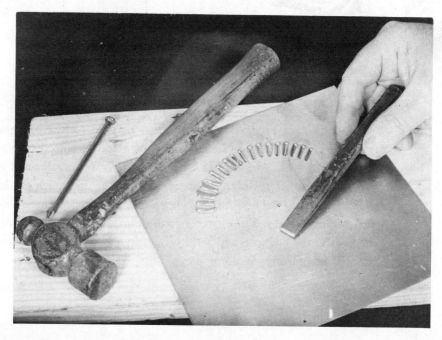

surfaces with molten solder. For instance, a spot on each end of the tin handle is covered with solder and the spots on the cup to which the handle is to be joined is also covered with solder. Then the tinned parts of the handle are connected with the tinned parts of the cup and the soldering iron is held there until the tin on the contiguous surfaces melts and joins. Then, with the handle still held in position (sometimes you can use wire to hold pieces until they are soldered), the soldering iron is removed and the solder allowed to cool and harden. If these directions are followed, soldering is delightfully simple.

After each job of soldering, wipe away all residue of the soldering paste with a rag soaked in alcohol or with fine steel wool.

28. A tin canister decorated with one of the brush strokes shown in 27.

29. A turntable is used to stripe a tin canister.

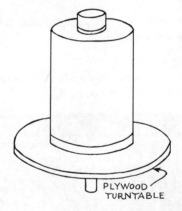

PLYWOOD TURNTABLE

A number of products and colors may be used for the background of freehand painting on tinware. If you want black, you need only give the tin one or two coats of flat black—Pittsburgh Waterspar Enamel No. 54-98, for instance. This leaves a sort of eggshell texture which can be given a slight sheen by rubbing briskly with a piece of folded cheesecloth after the surface has dried for twenty-four hours. This particular flat black enamel has the advantage of setting quickly enough to eliminate the dust problem completely. Some of the old-time tin painters used a japanned surface (asphaltum paint) for their backgrounds. However, unless you are producing a showpiece which will lead a sheltered life, this covering is not durable enough.

Dull red or vermilion was used as a background color, but here the choice for the painted design creates a difficult problem of contrast. Many pieces also had yellow, green, or buff backgrounds. An excellent effect is obtained by tinting flat white with umber. The japan color mixtures mentioned in this chapter are good for backgrounds of almost any color.

A great deal of the New England tinware, especially that made in Berlin, Connecticut, by Oliver Filley, the most prolific of all producers (he employed scores of women decorators and later established a Pennsylvania branch), was decorated with stencils in gold and transparent colors. The technique was exactly the same as that described in Chapter 12. However, many of the designs were so intricate that they would deter the beginner of today. Other workers occasionally used simple motifs such as the eagle (in solid gold color) in 26. The eagle was popular in the latter part of the Federal period, the 1820's.

In our opinion, however, the most charming pieces of old tinware, much of it from Pennsylvania, involved freehand brush-stroke painting. This may be a cause for concern to those who have no faith in their ability to draw or paint, but they are advised to withhold a verdict until they have read the instructions to follow.

But first a word about the necessary materials. These consist of three water-color brushes of different sizes—Nos. 2, 3, 6—a few ounces of

30. Authentic stenciled decoration taken from a 125-year-old tin nutmeg box made in Berlin, Connecticut.

turpentine (for cleaning brushes), a soapstone pencil for drawing the design on the painted tinware, some clean rags, and a few old saucers for mixing paints.

Aside from the flat enamel already described, or any other background colors preferred, you will need some tubes of japan colors. Do not make the mistake of buying pigments ground in oil, many of which are transparent. Tubes of japan colors are labeled accordingly and are all opaque. Perhaps five colors will be sufficient—vermilion, green (light and dark), blue, and yellow. This may seem to be a gaudy array to those of you who are unfamiliar with authentic old painted tinware, but brilliant color never fazed a Pennsylvania housewife.

The ground japan colors are mixed with equal parts of spar varnish and japan drier. After the japan color is added, your mixture should have the consistency of ordinary enamel. Be sure to mix the paint so that it will not weep or run.

If your colors seem too loud for your taste, you can get a toned-down, antique effect by mixing a bit of burnt umber with clear spar varnish and painting it over the entire surface after the article has been decorated. You may then reduce the sheen of the varnish by going over it lightly with fine steel wool and, finally, gently rubbing in furniture wax. If you are happy with the colors as they are, use the same procedure to finish the piece, omitting the burnt umber.

LVIII. Old tin pieces representing a haul from a farm auction, at a total cost of 10 cents. Each is perfect for painted decoration.

LVIX. A tin tinker's tool set; snips, ruler, dividers scriber (compass), chisel, hammer, tinsmith's hammer, wooden mallet, plain wire solder, and soldering iron (foreground).

LX. Tinware fashioned from old tin cans. The burner is from a discarded oil lamp.

LXI. A tin-plate dough tray purchased at a country auction and hand-decorated by Miss Katherine Worden, craftswoman of Lockport, New York.

LXII. Early tin candle sconce redecorated with a hand-painted floral.

LXIII. A home-made lantern fashioned from tin cans and dressed up with perforations produced by a large nail.

In applying the burnt-umber-and-varnish mixture, make certain you do not add too much umber. A too-light mixture is better than a too-dark one, which cannot very well be remedied except by wiping away completely with a turpentine-soaked rag. If, on the other hand, the antiquing is not deep enough, you can go over the surface again with slightly more umber added to the varnish. Mixing the umber with the varnish will be greatly facilitated if the umber is first diluted with turpentine and then added to the varnish. Stirring is continued until the tone is uniform. Very little oil color is needed for the small measure of varnish required to cover any one of the small articles mentioned here.

Of course, if you are not sticklers for authenticity, this work may be done with the ordinary colored enamels sold in small cans. After each painting, too much high gloss can be removed by an application of fine steel wool.

Beginners without art experience of any kind are advised to finish a few practice pieces before they embark on a real job. These may be on plywood panels covered with dull black varnish or any other background color. You may experiment with design on paper until you arrive at something that not only suits your fancy but conforms with the authentic product of over a century ago. A careful examination of the illustrations in this chapter will help to guide you.

Illustration 27 shows all the standard strokes used in brush stroke painting. Beginners should practice these strokes on paper until they achieve some competence. Much depends upon the pressure on the brush. Heavy pressure spreads it for maximum coverage, for instance. Thus, if you start with heavy pressure and a spread brush and reduce the pressure as you move the brush along, you will have a tapered streak of paint. By using these simple strokes you may get many variations of design.

We have not space to explore fully the ramifications of design as related to early nineteenth century decorated tinware. While a few examples are given in the photographs, they by no means cover the authentic variety. If your town has even a modest library, you will find at least one book on Pennsylvania Dutch folk art in which you will discover enough new material to satisfy your needs. Many of the old pieces showed the tomato ("love apple" in those days) as a central motif. Others used various combinations of brush-stroke painting easily duplicated.

LXIV. Old-time footwarmer and fire carrier decorated by a punch. (From the authors' collection)

LXV. An authentic lantern with an elaborate perforated design made by a chisel and punch. (From ·the authors' collection)

LXVI. Right. A fine example of tinware decoration of the 1820's. (From the collection of Miss Katherine Worden)

As we have said, japanned tinware is merely tinware covered with asphaltum paint, an old concoction still available at any paint store. Although ordinarily called black, it is really a deep brown. Dilution results in a light, rich brown. The color is produced by mixing two parts of asphaltum with one part spar varnish and one part turpentine. A very light golden color is the result of a mixture of one part asphaltum and one part turpentine. In all cases, asphaltum should be given plenty of time for drying; then apply a coat of spar varnish.

Japanned tinware was often decorated with plain gold or bronze powder, the designs or motifs applied with the help of a stencil. (See Chapter 12.) Simple 24-karat gold effects may be obtained by using Golden Touch sheets, mentioned elsewhere. These are applied directly to the protective coating of spar varnish over the asphaltum paint. The spar varnish should be completely dry, because the gold sheet is a sort of transfer. After the gold leaf has been applied and has dried for half an hour, it should in turn be covered with two coats of spar varnish. Decorative forms can be cut directly from Golden Touch sheets. Simply draw the object on the paper back of the sheets and cut out the forms with scissors. Not all old tinware was decorated with paint. Tin lanterns, foot warmers, and other articles were adorned with perforations made by chisel and punch, as several of the illustrations show. The design was first laid out on the flat tin plate with a straightedge, a compass, and a scriber. The tin plate was then laid on a block of soft wood and the chisel or the nail (or both) was hammered until it pierced the metal at the points indicated for the design. Lanterns decorated in this way supplied a surprising amount of light and also protected the candles from the wind.

Yesterday's Stenciling for Today's Furniture

{ 12 }

Stenciling in the form of the charmingly naïve decoration produced during the first half of the nineteenth century was by no means a home-practiced hobby. The old craft has been revived as such during the past twenty years, but it was most widely used in a purely American form on articles of furniture and tinware while Andrew Jackson was President of the United States. So-called "fancy furniture" of all types was stenciled; chairs, beds, chests, stands, and mirrors, and clocks of Terry, Jerome, and Hoadley (to mention but a few) were sent to market with the gaudy but still-acceptable form of mechanically produced painting. Sixty years passed before the vogue expired, and during this long period, professional stencilers, both male and female, were as numerous as shoemakers.

As beginners, you should curb any desire to work in the more advanced forms of stenciling on furniture. They offer a challenge, but unforeseen difficulties lead to despair. Rather, start with simple forms on practice panels of plywood (in 12 x 12-inch squares) until you master the rudiments and get the feel of the business.

The stencil in its simplest form amounts only to the outline of an object or a design cut into paper, placed over the article (wood, tin, glass, etc.) and the form or opening painted or dabbed with metallic or other powders on a still tacky varnish.

All stencils should be cut with sufficiently wide borders if you are to avoid staining the unstenciled surfaces with flecks of metallic powder. Stencils cut in the center of a relatively large piece of stencil paper offer a great deal of protection.

Perhaps the first stencil used need be nothing more than a piece of oiled or greased stencil paper—for instance, a tough grade of wrapping that has been previously dipped in hot paraffin—with a 2-inch circle cut out of the center.

Tracing linen used by draftsmen makes excellent material with which to cut stencils, especially if they are to be used repeatedly. The highly glazed surface does not readily adhere to tacky varnish. This material is also excellent for tracing off old stencils for reproduction. After the tracings have been completed, you can immediately set about cutting the stencils.

The practice panels of plywood should be well sandpapered, shellacked, and painted over with dull or flat black. After they are dry, take the panels, one by one as you need them, and cover one side with a good grade of spar varnish. One coat is enough; the actual stenciling is not started until the varnish is tacky enough to leave a fingerprint when a finger is pressed gently on the surface. Time required will depend upon the brand of varnish and the humidity and heat present. If the fingertip carries away varnish with it after the pressing test, then the varnish is still too wet to proceed with stenciling.

When the proper condition of tackiness is reached, lay the stencil with the circular opening on the panel and proceed to apply the metallic powder, which may be one of a number of shades of gold or plain silver or aluminum. Inasmuch as the stencil paper is oiled, there will be no danger of this sticking to the tacky varnish. The best quality of this metallic powder used for stenciling furniture is obtainable from the local paint shop or artcraft store.

A small amount of the powder, whatever it may be, is placed on a piece of glass and picked up in small amounts with a piece of velvet placed over the top of the index finger. In this way the powder is applied to the tacky varnished surface and then pressed into the varnish firmly and with a slight rotating motion which tends to produce a burnished or polished effect that increases luster and life. For the first panel, try to cover the entire circular opening as evenly as possible.

All excess metal powder should be brushed away both from the varnished surface and from the stencil itself before the stencil is removed. Otherwise a disastrous rain of powder will speckle the tacky surface when the stencil is lifted, a most disheartening calamity for which the only remedy is starting all over again on a fresh surface. These metallic pow-

ders are so light and so fine as to be easily air-borne. Wipe carefully with a clean rag moistened with turpentine.

If the first stencil has been cut on a piece of glass with a very sharp knife, a nice clean outline should be left when the stencil is finally lifted from the surface. If the knife was dull and the paper cut before it was prepared with paraffin (regular stencil paper already prepared may be had at art shops and paint stores), a fuzzy outline will be left due to the fibers of the paper that were pulled out rather than being cut with the knife. The fuzzy outline is the mark of the non-meticulous stenciler.

All stencils on old-time furniture depended a great deal upon shading and bleeding effects for their charm. Therefore, your second practice panel with the same circular stencil may be aimed at this effect. In place of solidly covering the opening in the stencil with powder, you cover only half, and from that point on you use gradually diminishing amounts of powder, working it out thinner and thinner until it bleeds off into pure black.

Although by no means a standard practice during days of yore, it is best that beginners place a thin second coat of spar varnish over a completed stencil. This will lock every particle of powder in place finally and

31. Copy of a stencil used on the slat of a Salem rocker during the mid-1820's.

protect the design from undue wear. Here, too, you will soon discover whether you have produced your design on a sufficiently tacky surface with the use of sufficient pressure and the careful wiping away of surplus powder. If you have not, woe be to you! Naturally, the varnish brush will pick up these loose remaining particles and distribute them over the solid backgrounds, a most unfortunate calamity without promise of effective remedy.

Before beginners become unduly confident and attempt to apply transparent oil colors over metallic powders, it is best once more to return to test panels where experience may be gained without heartache. Better to spoil a few panels rather than a chair over which you have patiently labored for hours. There is really no need to stencil new test panels; you can turn to the better of the panels previously done and proceed in the following manner:

Assemble the materials you will need. For coloring stencil designs you should have a kit comprised of the following: 5 tubes of oil-paint colors containing alizarine crimson, burnt umber, Prussian blue, raw umber, and yellow lake. Also, a piece of glass for a palette, a few small brushes, wads of cotton batting, a bottle of turpentine, and a small amount of good spar varnish.

For mixing, place a small amount of varnish on a glass or old china plate—this may be thinned a bit with turpentine. Then add a touch of, say, Prussian blue and mix it with the varnish. To soften the color further, add a mite of burnt umber. The umbers are added mostly to soften the other colors. The consistency of the varnish-turpentine-oil color combination is most important, for a mixture with a body about like house paint is needed.

Most workers experienced in applying color to stencils prefer first to cover the portion being worked upon with clear varnish of the same grade as that in which the colors are to be mixed. This makes for easier blending and bleeding or shading-off effects.

We might warn you that such oil colors as those mentioned above, even when mixed with relatively fast-drying spar varnishes, are themselves slow driers. Usually forty-eight hours or more are required for the varnish to reach a safe stage.

It would be well to spend a whole afternoon or evening mixing colors and creating desirable tones before risking actual color applications to a finished piece of work. You might also try bleeding-off or shading effects with your brushes and the clean cotton while you are experimenting with the color-mixing. There will be practically no need for the use of solid color.

When you have completed the stenciling of a chair or other article, you may apply a final coat of spar varnish. After this has thoroughly dried, go over it gently with fine steel wool, after which a coat of furniture wax is applied. While it is quite true that this procedure does have a tendency to dull the stenciled designs, this may come as a welcome relief to those striving for an antique effect.

This just about covers the essentials of stenciling. What remains to be learned cannot be taken from books; it must, rather, come from experience. It should also be pointed out here that the techniques described above are used no matter what is being stenciled: furniture of any kind, clock-glass borders, or the type of tinware made so popular during the years between 1825 and 1850. Stenciled tin trays were especially popular during these years. The decoration of such trays or other articles of tin is, with one exception, accomplished by the methods outlined above. The exception,

LXVII. Fruit-and-compote stencil on the slat of an 1820 side chair.

LXVIII. Fancy Hitchcock chair stenciled with fruit and leaves.

purely optional, is that of using a black japan rather than a dull black base upon which to place the stenciling. Black japan really amounts to nothing more or less than asphaltum paint, obtainable at any paint shop. This was the background material used exclusively by the largest painted tinware manufacturer of them all, Oliver Filley, who established his factory at Berlin, Connecticut, and who employed many women decorators highly skilled in the painting and stenciling of all kinds of tinware: flat trays of various shapes, both small and large, bread trays, cash boxes, candle boxes and sticks, canisters, coffee pots, sconces, etc. Hundreds of thousands of such gaily decorated work were carried about the northern United States by the slick Yankee peddlers. Many are the old attics even today that yield a piece or two of Filley tinware.

32 and 33. Floral stencils from the Cutting Collection of the Metropolitan Museum of Art.

It is also to be noted that blank trays ready for painting or stenciling are now being sold by artcraft and hobby stores. They are offered in various shapes and sizes.

If these are not available, there is always a supply of cheaply and gaudily finished trays at the local chain store. Such finishes are usually within easy reach of the modern paint removers, so that with very little work you may soon have a perfectly clean tray upon which to try your skill.

The stenciled tray design shown in 35 is of a type that was very popular during the 1820's, when the American Eagle was one of the most widely used Federal motifs; the Federal era, so called, came to a close in 1830.

A word about the application of asphaltum paint over which such a gold eagle might be placed. The tray must be scrupulously clean, having been washed and scrubbed with warm water and a pure soap. This is followed by a thorough warm-water rinsing and drying. Not less than three coats of the asphaltum paint should be used, with careful note of the drying periods recommended by the manufacturer on the can label.

Except in the case of very small designs, few indeed were the components of stenciled decorations that were solid color. All large leaves—the maple, for instance—were shaded. It usually happened that when the components were too small for shading, such as the stems of flowers, they will filled in solid.

After having satisfactorily completed several test panels to learn shading, use the rest of the blank panels to try progressively complicated designs, that is, designs requiring two or more stencils. Many of the old-timers used as many as ten stencils in their creations, each one being applied according to a definite sequence. For instance, in a floral group, you would have the petals and leaves, which might require the use of four stencils, as well as a stencil for the stems, each stencil to be applied in its proper order. If you wished to use the very old motif of a compote

34. The common thistle was used extensively as a motif for stenciling in the 1830's.

35. Copy of a stencil taken from a piece of furniture made in the 1830's.

filled with fruit, you might need seven or eight stencils, depending upon the number of pieces and the variety of fruits. The old-timers used peaches, pears, plums, grapes, melons, strawberries, etc. If you cut a stencil for each, you will have seven, including the compote, and still be without leaves and stems.

Of course, with multipiece stencils of this kind there is great scope for wide variety of arrangement. Each time you "fill" the compote, it can be done differently. Certainly once the stencils for this sort of design are cut there is no need to use all of them each time a design is laid. Infinite variety is, therefore, possible. More than one stencil was sometimes cut for each variety of fruit. There would be stencils for full grapes and half or quarter grapes, and so on. These sectional stencils came in handy for arranging compotes.

Many of the very early stenciled American chairs (1805-1820) were combinations of hand painting and stenciling. For instance, in the center of the top slat of a chair one might find a hand-painted sea or landscape with the rest of the decoration in orthodox stenciling. The same idea was carried out for some twenty years on shelf clocks, with the clock glasses always hand-painted.

Rare were the early stencils wholly without naturalistic motifs involving fruit, flowers, or shells, which were invariably used with appropriate designs with solid filling. Later on the choice of motifs widened considerably to include such things as certain animals (deer, for instance), ships, buildings, and birds. Borders and bandings took many forms, combinations of dots and dashes, repeated sections of leaves, etc.

Some of these old designs were highly intricate and multicolored, depending upon the type of trade for which the furniture was made. Aside from gold and silver, stencilers also employed transparent oils of green, blue, and yellow set against not only backgrounds of black but also of yellow, green, gray, and others. Although many modern workers use solid black for background, solid black was rarely used in the old days. It was more typical of the times that—in the case of chairs as an example —the black was placed over a basic coat of a sort of brick or Chinese red. While the black coating placed over the dry basic coating was still wet, narrow streaks of it were brushed away making the red underneath show through—a sort of graining effect to simulate rosewood.

36. A 6-unit stencil comprising right and left sprig of leaves, a right and left melon, a group of plums, and a compote.

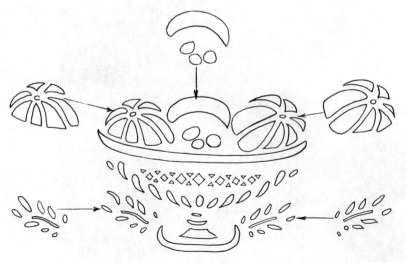

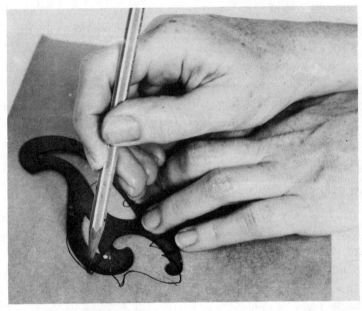

LXIX. In drawing designs for stencils on stenciling paper, the worker is greatly aided by the use of a French curve.

LXX. The application of bronze or gold powder to the tacky varnish of an article to be stenciled. The index finger is covered with velvet or chamois.

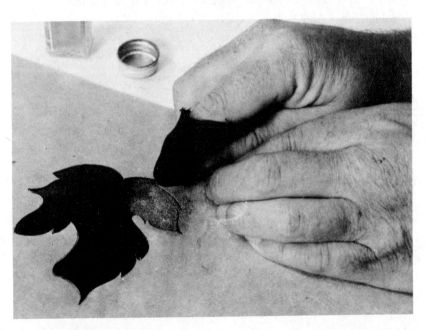

LXXI. A skilled craftsman striping and stenciling fancy chairs similar to those of the early 19th century. (*Courtesy Hitchcock Chair Co., Riverton, Connecticut*)

Nor were the borders of designs that were always set in panels or splats or slats of chairs always fancy. In the cheaper grades of furniture they were more apt to be straight lines of varying widths. Sometimes this striping was done in colored varnish by hand and sometimes in gold powder by means of a stencil. The latter method is recommended to the amateur who has never used a striping brush.

The remaining portion of this chapter will be devoted to the application of a reasonably complicated stencil to a chair of the 1830's.

If the chair comes to us with paint already on it, the question arises: should the old paint be removed or should we proceed to paint over it? Much will depend upon the condition of the old paint. If the old paint consists of several layers of paint placed one over the other during the long years, then there can be only one answer: complete removal down to the wood, followed by sanding and shellacking with still more sanding, after which you apply the red basic paint or, if you wish to have a plain black, then black paint. The basic coat of red is usually made up of Venetian red in japan drier, which will be pretty thin and must be applied with care if excessive weeping and running is to be avoided. When being applied, it is advisable to work on horizontal surfaces by turning the chair around as you proceed. For those who do not wish to work with such a thin mixture, it is entirely permissible to add spar varnish to it.

After the dull black has been applied over the red, and while it is very wet, proceed to remove some of it in such a manner that narrow streaks of red will show through. This may be done with a small dry brush, a rubber graining device, or even with the fingers. In any event, you do not wish to expose the red fully, but simply to permit some of it to peek through the surface of black so that the effect will be brownish rather than a full red.

Naturally, the top coating of black should be hard before the spar varnish is applied to function as the adhesive for the stenciling. Also, remember to apply the spar varnish bit by bit as needed, covering only the section to be worked upon immediately. If you varnished the whole chair at once, you would find that parts of it were far too hard to hold the powders when they were applied. Thus, always varnish a small area at a

LXXII. An 1820 tin tray stenciled over a japanned surface.

time. Every operation must be timed nicely whenever the varnish is involved.

As for the actual application of the stencil, little can be added to the instructions given for the finishing of the test panels. As far as shading is concerned, a great deal will have to rest with your artistic judgment, although it may be said that you should avoid solid sections as much as possible. For instance, the form of a peach solidly filled in with gold would be uninteresting and inaccurate, giving no indication of the line dividing the two halves of the peach.

Fancies with a Fret Saw

{ 13 }

Unlike the ladies, Victorian gentlemen were not long on hobbies—that is, not until fret or scroll saws began to appear in the hardware stores during the late 1850's. Then, surprisingly, thousands of men took off to the wood-shed workshops and began to saw up walnut at a rate never equaled since. For twenty years they kept at it, producing fancy picture frames, wall pockets, newspaper racks, what-nots, and bracket shelves. During the 1860's the hobby of fret-sawing was so popular that the lumber yards stocked specially cut walnut board ¼ to ⅛ of an inch thick. Little did those gentlemen know that some day their work would be sought after by collectors. Today a modest shelf may bring as much as $10, an elaborate what-not ten times that amount.

At present, fret or scroll saws are being put to use in reviving the hobby of the 1800's. And why not? A fine scroll saw may be bought for a few dollars, and thin plywood with walnut veneer is far more satisfactory than the thinly sliced walnut used a century ago. Plywood is easily sawed and is far stronger.

The craftsman in this medium has many designs from which to choose; he may find them in antique shops or he may get printed collections ready to trace off on wood. The Jig Saw Guild, c/o Home Craftsman Magazine, 115 Worth Street, New York, N.Y., supplies these. However, the ambitious craftsman can make himself independent of all sources of Victorian design. If he exercises his talent, he needs only a French curve or two, a sharp, soft pencil, and a piece of paper. Once he has produced a scrolled design that pleases him, he redraws it to the proper size and attaches it directly to the surface of the plywood to be used.

The best fret- or scroll-sawing is done at low speed. The coarser the

LXXIII. T w o scrolled bracket shelves cut with a fret saw, one modern and one about 90 years old.

LXXIV. A small masterpiece of delicate fret sawing made in 1868 with beechwood and framed. (From the authors' collection)

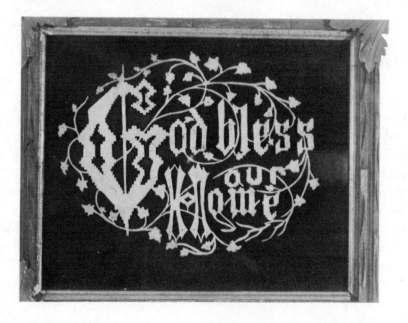

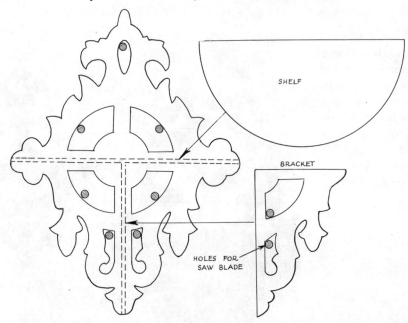

37. Fret-saw design. Such designs are first drawn on paper and then pasted to the wood to be cut. The holes noted are drilled to permit the entrance of the saw blade, which must be removed from the saw frame and replaced each time an inside section is to be cut out.

saw blade, the faster one may saw, but the penalty for speed is a ragged edge. It is best to purchase the finest blades obtainable, with the most saw teeth per inch.

If you have not used the fret saw before, study illustration 37. You will notice that a number of ⅛-inch holes have been drilled through the piece before sawing. A hole should be drilled in each inside section to be sawed out. Begin by removing the saw blade from the saw frame, thread it through the hole and replace it in the frame. After the piece is sawed out, the operation is repeated in reverse. So it goes for every section to be removed. As in all other types of sawing, downward pressure is placed on the saw blade on the forward stroke and released on the return stroke. However, a scroll saw blade is rather delicate, and you may break several before you discover the proper procedure. Saw blades are inexpensive, and a few accidents will not be very costly.

Clean sawing comes of using not only the finest blade, but also of

LXXV. Milady tries her hand at fret sawing during the 1860's.

LXXVI. At the height of the fret-sawing
craze during the late 1860's, manufacturers
supplied this foot-propelled machine
equipped with a treadle.

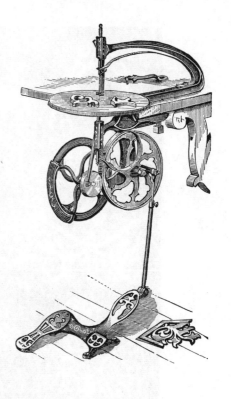

having a firm grip on the wood. Above all, avoid the vibration which is
bound to happen when the wood is not held tightly in a vise. A firm hold
in the vise—without, however, running the risk of bruising the surface of
the wood—is best accomplished by tying felt (perhaps from an old hat)
over the jaws of the vise or covering them with soft pine blocks. Only
enough vise pressure to hold the work is needed. Avoid sawing too far
away from the jaws of the vise, because heavy vibration will set up beyond
a certain distance. Constantly move the work in such a way that, as sawing
proceeds, you are always working a short distance from the spot held. With
reasonable care, this guarantees a clean line. In fret-saw work you may
need one or more duplicates of certain pieces. If so, use the first piece as a
master to trace the design from.

38. Left. During the 1870's, A. H. Shipman of Rochester, New York, manufactured a line of fret saws for hobby use and supplied printed patterns of the correct size, which were simply glued to the thin wood to be sawed. These are some of the choices illustrated in his catalog.

39. Mr. Shipman warned that only experienced fret sawyers should order his pattern of the Lord's Prayer.

LXXVII. An example of more ambitious fret sawing, done from ⅜-inch oak, side and front views.

.   No matter how fine the saw blade, the careful workman will not be satisfied with the edges of the work as they are. You should go over them with ooo sandpaper cut in strips and glued to ¼-inch and ⅛-inch dowels. Hold the wood in the vise while sandpapering the edges.

The problem of finishing or varnishing the edges, to match the veneered surface, is one that requires some thought. You may not realize this until you see the contrasts between them after a bit of sawing. It has been the authors' experience that walnut oil stain offers the best solution. Apply it to the edges with a small brush and wipe it off after a minute or so. If the edges are still too light, let the stain stand for a while longer before you wipe away the excess.

Some fret-sawing was extremely delicate and gossamerlike, as may be seen in 38 and 39. Only the highly skilled devotees of the craft were capable of sawing thin wood—often much less than $\frac{1}{8}$-inch thick—so intricately. Such workers sometimes sawed the wood into Biblical quotations or mottoes for framing.

If you are brave enough to try some really fine fret-sawing, you may find these suggestions helpful. The real difficulty lies in the danger of breaking the wood when cutting out the smallest sections of a design. The drag of the saw blade often causes this. Hence, it is advisable to work very close to the jaws of the vise and to keep moving the wood section even closer than usual to the vise jaws. Experts use two pieces of plywood instead of one to provide more backbone for the wood and, of course, to cut two pieces at once. The Victorian craftsmen often cut small trinket shelves in pairs. For cutting two pieces of wood back-to-back simultaneously, the wood should be larger than the pattern requires, say one inch oversize. This margin allows you to nail or glue together the edges of the wood pieces temporarily while sawing.

Preserving Nature's Flora Inside the House

{ 14 }

Nearly a hundred years have passed since the Reverend Edward Huber's article on drying flowers was published in the *Ladies' Floral Cabinet*. Not that the hobby of drying flowers was new at the time; European ladies had been doing it long before the craft was introduced to America. In Germany it had even become commercially attractive. Bouquets of treated flowers were made not only for the home market, but also for export, to delight ladies in London, Paris, and Rome.

The Reverend Huber had experimented long and patiently with the process before he saw fit to pass on his secrets to the Victorian ladies here. We have gleaned his directions from the brittle, yellow pages of the *Cabinet*.

Flowers undergo the drying process with different results. Most suffer little change; others change greatly, especially in color, but all will last the winter out. According to Huber, scabiosa, pinks, forget-me-nots, honeysuckle, pansies, and sweet peas are easily dried. On the other hand, tulips, hyacinths, and other flowers with a thick, full corolla are to be avoided.

The essentials are simple enough: a cigar box, a few pounds of *fine* sand (just enough to fill the box), and a few ounces of stearin, which may be the kind of tallow candle used by plumbers. For preparation, the sand is placed on trays or in shallow dishes and set in an oven at low heat for several hours. During the last hour of heating, the temperature of the oven should be increased so that the sand is hot enough to melt the tallow shaved off the candle onto it. The sand is then poured into an iron kettle over an open gas flame for further heating.

The object now is to mix the dry sand with molten tallow thoroughly. To accomplish this, continue to shave the candle onto the sand, stirring intermittently with an old spoon until the whole sand mass is impregnated. This step calls for patience, the secret of success in most hobbies.

The cigar box into which the warm sand and flowers are to be placed should be prepared ahead of time by boring several well distributed ½-inch holes in the bottom and then gluing a piece of heavy wrapping paper over the entire bottom of the box. (The sand is drained off later through the holes. By puncturing the paper covering the holes, the sand sifts through and you do not have to dig the brittle flowers out by hand.)

Now for the business of encasing the flowers in the warm, treated sand. Use a flour sifter to cover the bottom of the box with about half an inch of sand and place the flowers to be dried on this bed. The flowers should not be moist from dew or rain and should have been allowed to dry a few hours in the sun. Continue sifting the sand over the flowers until they are completely covered. The trick here is to see to it that the sand reaches down into the petals of the blossoms. Packing or pressing with the fingers is unwise because of the danger of bruising and distortion. You can solve the problem by tapping the sides of the box and dipping it back and forth to guide the sand into corners and pockets that it might not otherwise reach.

After the flowers have been covered, another layer is set in place and the process repeated. The next step is to keep the box in a warm place for three to four days before the sand is drained off the bottom. (The Reverend Huber had a baker keep his box on top of the oven in the bakery.) In the summertime, the attic is an ideal place for drying flowers. In winter, you might place the box on top of, or at least near, the furnace for about four days.

The Reverend Huber warned against trying to remove the dried flowers if they are brittle enough to break. He recommended that the box, minus the sand, be left in a cool moist place—a cellar or ditch—for several days. Since ditches are scarce in American cities, we suggest a large cardboard box in a cool cellar with a pan of water in it. Those living in apartments will have to make a deal with the janitor. (If he appears a bit incredulous, just tell him you're crazy and let it go at that!)

If we indulge in Victorian pastimes, we get used to the fact that the various moods of nature ranked high with the artcrafters in those days. If they were not modeling flowers in wax, or even leather, they were dyeing grass, thistles, or leaves, or crystallizing them in saturated solutions of alum. We do not know who developed and sponsored this fascinating hobby that was widely practiced in the 1860's.

The so-called crystallization of flowers, leaves, and grasses amounts simply to suspending specimens in super-saturated solutions of alum in water. Within a few hours, the alum deposits itself upon the specimens in icelike formations, simulating the hoar frost of a January morning. The super-saturated solution is nothing more or less than a solution made with hot water. Let the hot water dissolve the alum until it will take no more—the hotter the water, the more the liquefaction. After this, as the water cools, crystals of alum deposit themselves on the walls of the container and its contents.

Flowers, grasses, leaves, or thistles to be covered with "crystallized diamonds," as one of the Victorian hobbyists put it, were hung in the alum solution, blossom or heavy end down, by means of small wires, the dry ends of which were wound around a small stick placed across the mouth of the jar or crock holding the solution. Naturally, the specimens were not immersed while the solution was still hot; to avoid destroying the blossom, wait until the solution has cooled.

This is not a quick process. Crystalline deposits of the alum do not begin to form on the specimens until at least five hours have passed. Victorian writers on the subject recommended that the specimens be left for at least fifteen hours, then removed and hung upside down to dry.

A quite different effect can be achieved if the drying is accelerated by placing the specimens before a fire. This has the effect of making the crystal appear white and snowlike. Although the authors have not had very much experience with the process, we feel that fast drying produces a much more beautiful effect; at least it did on the pussy willows we tried.

Crystallized flowers and leaves made up a large part of what the Victorian ladies called their "winter bouquets." These were carefully prepared in late summer or early fall and, as likely as not, discarded late the following spring. Popular also as a component of such bouquets was colored grass.

First the grass leaves (or any other leaves, for that matter, although response to bleaching varies) had to be bleached in a simple solution of chlorinated lime, or chloride of lime as it is more frequently called. Two teaspoonfuls of this are moistened and mashed to remove all lumps. This is dissolved in a quart of water to which two teaspoonfuls of acetic acid is added. Strain the solution through muslin or other clean cloth and it is ready for use.

The chlorophyl of most vegetable matter has been pretty well bleached out after a 10- or 15-minute exposure. Remove the specimens and rinse them thoroughly in running water just as you would wash a photographic negative. Then place them between clean white blotting paper and put them under pressure until they are dry. The dyeing itself is quite easy.

In Victorian days, women often used natural dyes such as Brazilwood, cudbear, cochineal, or anetta in "spirituous solution" (any of the alcohols). But in place of cochineal, cudbear, or sumac, today there is a wide choice of colors at the local drugstore in the form of aniline dyes such as those used for fabrics. Tints or solid colors may be used as you like.

LXXVIII. The Reverend Huber method of drying flowers. Hot, treated sand is sifted over the specimens and the box set away for several days.

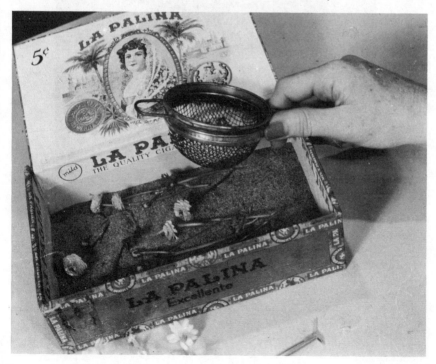

Mrs. C. S. Jones, editor of the *Ladies' ·Floral Cabinet* and one of the best-known artcraft writers and instructors of her day, outlined her own process for dyeing flowers in 1868. Since we have had no experience in this, we quote Mrs. Jones:

"When the everlasting flowers (or *Immortelles* of the French) are of a homely color, it is desirable, perhaps, to dye them some pleasing shade; or, again, as they are generally in a natural state, of only a few colors, such as yellow, rose and white, and a variety is desirable in a collection, it is customary, in Europe, especially, to resort to coloring as a means of imparting brightness and beauty to a bouquet, or other 'arrangement' of these flowers.

LXXIX. Many Victorian parlors boasted of a "winter bouquet" made of either crystallized or dried flowers.

"The Ammobium, white Acroclinium, Pearly Everlasting, Xeranthemum of one kind, and the white Gomphrena, are colorless in themselves, and, with some little preparation of cleansing, may be dyed without bleaching, or fading. Those which require the color changed must be placed in a solution of Castile (white) soap and warm water, with a little borax added, to an ounce and a half of shaved soap, putting one quart of water and a piece of borax as large as a filbert. Place the flowers in this while it is boiling hot, keeping them upon the stove for a half hour or so; then rinse in cold, clear water, repeating the process until the color is removed.

"White flowers and grasses may be dyed with the aniline dyes, as before mentioned; or, for some shades, Brazil-wood, cudbear, cochineal, anetta, and other old-fashioned dyes may be used, but will not prove so clear and brilliant as the former. Some, too, may have the natural colors changed, spotted, striped, etc. by using acids, alum, lye and other agents, and for some touches of transparent colors, produce fine effects. In using the aniline dyes, all that is required is to mix the liquid or powder with boiling water, and soak the flowers or grasses in this until sufficiently dyed; or proceed according to the directions upon the package, substituting the flowers, etc., instead of the silk or other fabric for coloring, which directions are printed."

Still another craft sponsored by Mrs. Jones, but as yet untried by the authors, is that of a process, new at that time, for preserving flowers for winter bouquets. Again we quote this acknowledged mistress of Victorian handicrafts:

"No doubt many of our readers have looked with admiration and wonder upon the chaplet or cross of pure white flowers, preserved as mementos of 'friends departed,' or as treasured relics of the day when some fair bride stood under the snowy 'marriage bell' and carried the lovely bouquet of orange blossoms, camellias, etc., which, within their glass cases, appear as perfect now as in the hour they were gathered.

"For many years the art by which these white flowers were preserved was kept a great secret, and only those belonging to the 'mystic circle' of the initiated understood the operation; and these reaped rich harvests from those wealthy persons who were willing to pay fabulous prices for the flowers that had rested on the breast of some loved, but departed friend, or graced the wedding of another loved one; but, by one of those accidents which, always in time, expose to light the long-entombed secrets of the wise ones, this interesting process has at last been made public; and we learn that the following process will enable anyone to preserve the white and green flowers used upon special occasions, or, perhaps, desired for their beauty of form of other attribute.

"Let the flowers be freshly plucked, and of those kinds which have firm texture, of pure white, or at least very delicate tints. If the collection is to be preserved without separating the parts, the green leaves must be removed, as they require a different treatment. This done, take fine paraffine, that is, of the very best quality, which melt in a clean, new tin vessel placed in a pan of boiling water, which must be kept constantly hot around it, so as to keep the paraffine in a liquid state. Into this thin and transparent liquid mass, dip the blossoms; or, if found more convenient, brush each one quickly with a soft camel's-hair brush of small size, so as to give them a smooth, thin coat that will cover every part of petal; and this will form a casing about them that will entirely exclude the air, and prevent their withering. The perfect transparency of the material renders this coating entirely invisible, so that the flowers present that natural appearance which constitutes the peculiar charm of this work.

"Green leaves must be coated with green wax, or with paraffine colored with green paint, in powder, tied in a thin, Swiss-muslin bag and melted in it. Chrome green is best, lightened to proper shade by the addition of chrome yellow; or, if a blue-green leaf is desired, permanent blue added in very small quantity.

"We have experimented in this, during the season, by coloring the paraffine with other colors, such as pink, lavender, etc., and have been quite successful with a certain class of flowers. Those fond of experimenting will find this a most interesting field in which to indulge their taste, as the flowers thus preserved are as perfectly natural as if freshly gathered.

"Great care is necessary in having the paraffine perfectly liquefied, yet not so hot that it will 'cook' the blossoms; for in this case, they will turn brown and 'sluff off'; that is, become soft and apparently decayed.

"We will now give still another process, which has been kept a matter of great secrecy, and, of course, excited a vast amount of curiosity in Europe for some years; but which the public periodicals in France and

England have been making public for a year or two past. The first flowers we saw preserved in this way was a wreath, in a deep recess frame, exhibited in the window of an art emporium in Chicago, in the year 1871, and we imagined at the first glance, that they were wax; but, upon examination, found they were natural flowers,—the tints rather lighter than in the fresh state; still, quite perfect in form, and exceedingly delicate and lovely in

LXXX. An autumn wreath made by pressing colored leaves, varnishing them, and tying them to a horseshoe-shaped frame of wire for hanging.

appearance. Upon inquiry, we were informed that they were imported, and were dried by the fumes of sulphur, though in what manner was not known. From that time on we felt greatly interested concerning the process, but had no opportunity of discovering anything more concerning the matter until some time after, when a scientific gentleman explained the process to us; and soon after, we read the same in different journals, and began to make an attempt to preserve a few simple flowers, as an experiment, since which, as we succeeded well, we have continued, increasing our collection; finding the process not only simple, but exceedingly interesting, we assure our readers they can also do it, if they will attempt it.

"The only articles necessary for this operation are a closed box, a pan for the sulphur, and some stick sulphur. Any tight wooden or tin box will answer, with a little preparation, made as follows: Supposing there are flowers sufficient to fill a half-peck basket; a wooden box, about two feet square is taken (we find one of the square tea-boxes convenient, as being light and easily handled, and also, because closely papered), and upon the inside, two strips screwed or nailed on opposite sides upon which the rods

LXXXI. An 1870 shadow box with dried flowers, leaves, and grasses.

holding the flowers are rested. As the box is air-tight, the ignited sulphur would speedily consume the small portion of air contained in the box, and be immediately smothered; it is necessary, therefore, to have a hole or two bored, or a little door with a hinge made in one end of the box, which may be opened or closed at pleasure, the former having plugs or corks fitting them tightly.

"Our course is this: Having selected a number of Roses and buds, Fuchsias, Dahlias, Larkspurs, Orange Flowers, Camellias, Pansies, etc., we tie them in loose clusters of from two to six or eight, according to size, and hang them upon rods, which fit across the box upon the ledges, placing about four rows of them. In an iron pan are some live embers of charcoal, which is set upon the bottom of the box; an ounce or two of crushed sulphur is sprinkled quickly over, and the lid, which, in our case, slides, pushed into place. The little panel or door, which is on the lower part of one side, and has a hinge, is held open for a few minutes until, glancing in, we perceive all is progressing favorably and the fumes are rising from the ignited sulphur, when we close and hook the door, which fits tightly. Throw a heavy blanket over the box, tucking it round closely and leave it until the following day, or about twenty-four hours, when they will, if all has gone well, be found bleached to a dull white color. This, upon exposing them to the air, in a dry atmosphere, they gradually lose, and assume their own colors, though not of such intense vivid shades, perhaps, as before bleaching, but permanent.

"It is of the utmost importance, in this operation, that the box be made perfectly tight and close by pasting muslin or paper over each corner; and if the lid closes down upon the top, to paste a strip around it also, as it can be easily cut open along the crack when the box is to be opened. Some bleaching-boxes are fitted with holes about an inch in diameter at top and bottom, fitted with corks, in order to admit the air; though we prefer the little door as being more convenient; and it consists in simply sawing out an inch square from the side of the box, fastening it in on the upper part with a hinge and below with a hook; it, of course, fits closely into the exact place from which it was sawed. Once the sulphur is ignited, the box should be kept as close as possible; as upon this depends the success of the operation, in a great measure.

"The room in which the box is placed should be as dry as possible, for in a damp atmosphere, the bleaching will not be accomplished so satisfactorily.

"Flowers, thus preserved, if well arranged, and sealed hermetically under a glass shade or behind a recess frame, will retain their beauty and perfection of form and color for an indefinite time."

A Harvest of Wax Fruit

{ 15 }

There was a bumper crop of wax fruit in mid-Victorian days. Dining-room tables were adorned with epergnes piled high with delicately colored wax apples, grapes, oranges, lemons, and peaches. Fashionable as these were, very few of them have been handed down to us. With changing customs, they were relegated to the trashbasket or to the attic where they soon lost their pristine bloom and contour beneath the warm eaves.

Anyone who would rather make than collect wax fruit is fortunate. Beginning in the 1850's, considerable literature was devoted to the subject. When we decided to try our hand at the business, we dug up several old books which described every step in the process. Especially informative was a book by J. E. Tilton and Co. of Boston, published in 1862. From this we selected the following directions which may be followed easily if one has a little patience and skill.

Wax fruit was cast in plaster-of-Paris molds. When you learn how to cast an orange or an apple, you can cast any fruit—lemons, cucumbers, or bananas. We will use an orange as an example.

The first venture requires very little material, all of it inexpensive and readily available. Any corner drugstore will supply a pound package of plaster of Paris for about 35 cents. You will also need a strip of tin about 3 inches wide. This tin is to be bent into a ring with a diameter great enough to leave 1 inch of space between it and the orange when it encircles the orange, plus a slight allowance for overlapping at the ends, illustration 40. These, with a coffee tin, three small marbles, a ruler, piece of string, large spoon, paint brush, some fine sand (the cleaner and finer, the better), wax, and coloring matter complete your list of tools and materials.

Fill the coffee can with moistened sand and level off the excess. Then

147

press the orange down into this sand (stem end up) until a little less than half of it is immersed in the sand. Pressing down the orange will, of course, displace some of the moist sand. This excess sand around the "equator" should be carefully leveled off a second time with a ruler edge.

Ready now to use the strip of tin, you bend it into a ring of such diameter that when it is placed over the orange, as shown in LXXXVI, there will be about an inch of space between the orange and the inside of the ring. Since you may be using this strip of tin again and again for this

LXXXII. The simple materials used in casting wax fruit.

purpose, you needn't solder the joint for the ring. Simply overlap the strip at the outside of the ring and fasten with string wound tightly and tied. Before actually inserting the ring, press the three small marbles half-way down into the moist sand around the orange; they should be set at equidistant intervals half the distance between the orange and the eventual position of the ring. The marbles play an important part. This plaster-of-Paris mold for the orange will be in two parts, and you are now making the first half. It is imperative that both halves of the mold come together perfectly; that is, they must line up. The marbles are put in place so that the first half of the mold cast will have three depressions left in it to guide you in making a two-piece mold that will fit together. Next, the tin ring is slipped over the orange and the marbles and is pressed down into the sand until only half an inch of the rim is exposed above the orange.

The mold set-up is now ready for pouring the plaster of Paris. In preparing and pouring it, you must work rapidly. Clean water is added to a few ounces of the plaster of Paris until it has a creamy consistency. If the amount is insufficient, you can quickly prepare more. Gently pour the mixture over the orange until the tin ring is filled to the top, completely covering the orange. Let the work stand until the plaster of Paris hardens enough so that a slight impression can be made with the finger. This requires only a few minutes.

Lift the whole thing out of the sand: ring, orange, and marbles. Cut the string and remove the plaster-of-Paris casting from the ring. The orange and marbles embedded in the mold can be easily removed, and you have a perfect plaster cast of marbles and orange. Some sand will cling to the

LXXXIII. Basket of wax fruit, including a slice of a melon (old favorite of the Victorian ladies) and a half of a peach.

plaster; it should be lightly brushed away. The surface to which the sand adhered can also be smoothed up with a knife if necessary. The plaster should still not be too hard to prevent doing this.

Preparation of the second half of the mold is much easier. Put the orange back into the first half of the mold as close as possible to its original position. Then, using a small brush, paint the edges of the first half of the mold, including the holes made by the marbles, with melted tallow or wax. This prevents the fresh plaster of Paris, used to cast the second half of the mold, from adhering.

With the stem end down, tightly encircle the orange with the tin strip and tie it firmly with a string. Pour prepared plaster of Paris over the orange as before. After it has hardened, insert the blade of a knife in the joint and separate the two parts, again removing the orange. The mold is now ready for use.

The wax itself may be ordinary paraffin, old candles, almost anything. However, take the precaution of melting the wax, whatever it may be, in a double boiler, or a serious fire may result. For fruit of a solid color, such

LXXXIV. An orange ready to cast in plaster of Paris. A coffee can is used to hold the sand.

LXXXV. The orange covered with plaster of Paris.

LXXXVI. The orange about to be removed from the plaster-of-Paris mold. The marbles also leave their impressions in the mold.

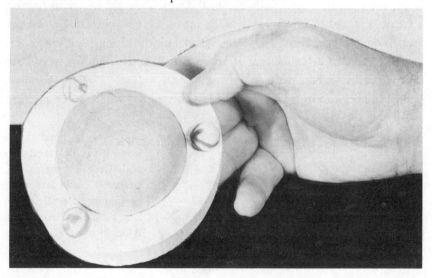

LXXXVII. The orange removed from the mold.

as oranges and lemons, the wax is colored before the casting is made. Add a little turpentine to any of the colors ground in oil or japan and pour the mixture into the wax while it is molten. Thorough stirring distributes the coloring matter uniformly throughout the wax. Colors may be mixed in the ordinary way—yellow and blue for green, et cetera, and, by and large, the color is carried faithfully to the wax. It might be useful to melt a bit of wax and to mix various colors into it before you actually cast the fruit. You may be surprised by the small amount of coloring matter needed.

Now, for the actual casting of an orange. Since it is hollow, very little wax is needed—about half an average candle will do. Preheat the mold before you begin casting. It should be left in very hot water for ten minutes

40. Casting a plaster-of-Paris mold for an orange or apple as described in the

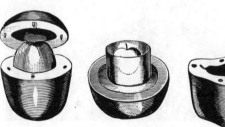

text. Fruit or vegetables with irregular shapes like pears or cucumbers must be laid horizontally while the plaster-of-Paris mold is being made.

to make sure that the heat has permeated it thoroughly. Thus, you prevent the wax from sticking to the surface when the orange is cast.

While the mold is being heated, you can melt the wax in the double boiler and stir in the color. The wax should be warm enough to insure sufficient fluidity. Then remove the mold from the hot water and carefully pat (not wipe) it dry with clean cheesecloth or other soft, absorbent fabric. Any attempt to wipe the mold dry inside will tend to destroy the natural irregularities of the orange cast into the surface of the plaster. Holding half of the still-hot mold in one hand, fill it three-quarters full of hot wax. Put the other half of the mold in place and press it down as tightly as possible to prevent leakage of the hot wax as you turn the mold slowly about in all directions. This slow turning allows the wax to congeal gradually on the inside walls of the mold. You can accelerate this process by turning the mold under cold water. At any rate, a few minutes of turning will deposit all of the wax. The mold can then be opened and the

LXXXVIII. Wax fruit in a wax basket. The basket shown above is made of wire repeatedly dipped in hot wax.

orange carefully removed. If the orange is at all soft (waxes vary in time required for hardening), immerse it in cold water before attempting to remove it from the plaster.

Excess wax will be attached to the orange around the middle at the joint of the mold. This can be cut or scraped off with a knife and the spot rubbed gently with a rag soaked in turpentine. No blemish should be left.

This is a beginning, although, as the authors' drawings of several molds indicate, not all are made the same way. Much depends upon the shape of the fruit or vegetable. Pears and cucumbers, for instance, have to be cased sideways, at right angles to their stems or axes. And while fruit of solid color presents no difficulties, bananas, apples, and peaches call for special talent and skill in tinting. Painters' oil colors may be mixed with clear varnish and applied to the wax fruit. The blush on the wax apple, grape, and peach, and so on, comes from finely powdered carmine dye brushed on much as a lady might rouge her cheeks.

LXXXIX. A realistic half of a peach cast in peach-colored wax, with a pit painted brown. The specimen illustrated was cast in the early 1860's.

XC. Wax fruit and vegetables in wholes and pieces. Melon sections were also popular during the height of the hobby, in the 1860's.

Flowers That Bloom in Wax

{ 16 }

Countless flowers of wax bloomed between 1860 and 1880 as parlor bouquets in shadow boxes or in glass domes on mantels. Some were "boughten" but most were made by the ladies of the household during the long winter evenings while Father read the paper or played dominoes with a neighborhood crony. Instructions were published in books and magazines, classes were formed in the larger cities, and materials became available not only at art and stationery stores but often at drugstores.

When we decided to investigate this now almost-forgotten hobby, we came upon a little book, *The Art of Modelling Flowers in Wax* published in 1864 by George Worgan. One Effie Clark of Brooklyn, New York, had owned it and had carefully itemized her expenses in the front of the book. They included twelve lessons at $1 each and $12.75 for materials which had been purchased at H. H. Dickinson's Pharmacy at Montague Place and Hicks Street. Fortunately, it costs much less to model flowers in wax today than it did ninety years ago. The authors' own expenses were well under $5.00.

When the craft of making wax flowers was very new (it can be traced back to the eighteenth century in England), one had to make and tint one's own wax sheets. During late Victorian times, however, the craft was so popular that ready-made sheet wax, clear or tinted, was manufactured and sold in the stationery and art stores. A brand made by Frau Scheiffele was imported from Germany and widely distributed. It came in single, double, and triple thicknesses and in a variety of colors, although workers still tinted white or clear wax themselves with powders sold for that purpose. This was required for flower petals that were not a solid color. Single thickness sheets were used for small, delicate flowers, double for lily pads.

156

The larger the petal or leaf, the thicker the sheet. The waxes and combinations of waxes used varied, but all manufacturers tried to produce sheets that would resist drying out and make the flowers brittle. Although we have searched diligently for these manufactured sheets, they are apparently no longer produced, at least in this country. Consequently, if you want to take a fling at flower-making, you will have to make your own wax sheets.

First, you make a small tin box into which the hot wax is poured for molding into a cake. This box should be about 1 inch high, 3 to 4 inches wide, and from 5 to 6 inches long. If possible the sides and ends of the box should be tapered a bit; that is, the top end of the box should measure a bit more than the bottom to permit the cool wax to fall out better. In any event, the inside of the box is greased with lard or vegetable shortening or ordinary lubricating oil before the hot wax is poured into it. This, too, will facilitate removal after the wax has cooled.

After the wax has cooled, the cake is ready for cutting into sheets. One method makes use of the tin box in which the wax was cast. The cake must first be removed, however. Then cut a few pieces of Bristol board just large enough to fit into the tin box (see illustration 42). If one piece of Bristol board is placed in the bottom of the box and the cake of wax placed over it, the top of the cake will rise over the edge of the box to a distance equal to the thickness of the Bristol board. Two pieces of Bristol board in the bottom of the box will double the amount of wax above the edges of the box.

Thus, by using a very sharp bread knife, slightly warmed (the wax should be warm, too—never cold), you may easily cut off wax sheets either very thick or very thin. One of the authorities on old-time wax-flower-making made his wax cakes smaller and used a carpenter's plane to cut his sheets.

A good source of ready-colored wax is found in candles. If the wax is first made into sheets as described and then formed into leaves or flowers, etc., while it is warm—not hot—it responds with comparative ease. Where solid colors without shading are needed, as in the case of green leaves, dark green candles offer a ready and cheap supply of material.

Among numerous wax combinations that may be used for flower-making is a 50-50 mixture of bleached (white) beeswax and cocoa butter. The mixture may be colored in a melted state or tinted later. If the wax is to be colored while it is in a melted state, an addition of aniline dye dissolved in alcohol will do the trick. It is clear that no color with water as a solvent can be mixed with wax of any kind not miscible with water. But as a rule, colors dissolved either in turpentine or in one of the alcohols are miscible with most waxes.

Shaded tinting can be accomplished with white wax in one of several ways. The transparent oil colors used for tinting photographs may be used when mixed with the solvents found in such kits and applied with a piece of soft cotton with slight pressure. Blending with the wax surface will be accelerated if the wax is slightly warmed.

All of the artist's oil colors, sold in tubes, may be thinned with turpentine and used to color any kind of molten wax. The amount of color used depends upon the depth of the color sought. Tinting requires very little. In any event, turpentine is added to the oil color and is well mixed, after which it is added to the molten wax.

There is no reason why ordinary paraffin cannot be used for making wax flowers just as it was for casting wax fruit. First melt the paraffin in a double boiler and mix with it a small amount of either color ground in oil (such as artists use) and turpentine or japan color and turpentine. Thus,

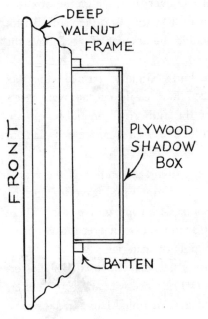

41. A shadow box suitable for mounting bouquets of wax flowers can be made easily by installing a small plywood box in the rear of a late-Victorian walnut picture frame.

42. *Opposite.* The Bristol board placed beneath a cake of wax in a box so that sheets may be cut. Th raises the wax above the top of t box, permitting a thin sheet to sliced off with a sharp, warm knife. greater thickness of the wax sheet required, 2 or 3 sheets of Bristol boa are placed beneath the cake of wa

if you are going to cut some leaves, there is no reason why you cannot make up a batch of green wax and cut it into small sheets as described. In any case, for solid colors, as in the modeling of daisies and black-eyed Susans, the same method is used. For pond or calla lilies buy the whitest candles you can find and melt them for sheets, or use paraffin. While the wax is in a molten state, simply add a little titanium-zinc white, ground in oil. This is sold in tubes like all artists' colors. We have also found that white lead ground in oil imparts a good opaque white to the same paraffin that is used for topping preserves and jellies.

Workers are warned against melting the wax directly over gas flames. Overheating with consequent fire is apt to result. A small double boiler for such work may easily be made from two tin cans, one fitting into the other. After the color is added, the mixture should be stirred thoroughly. The temperature of the wax is important. Work with cold wax, no matter how skillfully done, will be very difficult if not impossible. Wax should be at least 85°F. preferably 95°F. while it is being worked upon and shaped into petals and leaves. These temperatures are easily maintained if we have a bowl-type electric heater or an infra-red lamp around the house. If this is set up a few feet away from the worker, he will have little trouble with brittle wax that is too cold to work.

In the old days, the suppliers did not overlook a single need of the wax flower hobbyist. Although not all workers used them, the art stores carried small leaf and petal cutters made of tag-plate, a very thin tin that could be cut with scissors. When a worker had to make extra-large bouquets of a single flower, he bought a sheet or two of tag-plate and made his own cutters. These worked just like mother's tin cookie cutters.

All of the old-timers who wrote about this craft warn beginners to

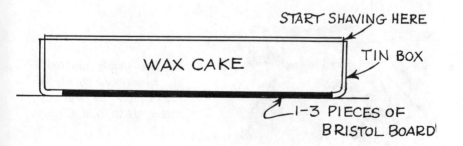

43. Tag tin (very thin) used to be sold to wax flower makers so that they could make their own cookie-type cutters to duplicate flower petals and leaves. (From *Making Wax Flowers*, 1862)

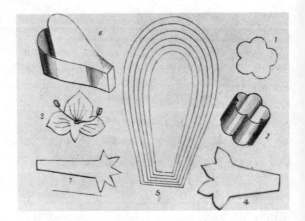

make the bottoms of their petals where they are attached to the stem with less of a curve than the natural petal has. Natural petals are attached to stems by a very small connection which would be far too small for wax flowers. What you want is a larger portion of the petal to be attached to the stem.

Up to the point of forming leaves and petals, the worker requires little talent or skill. From this point onward, however, the project is more demanding if you are to wind up with something worthy of being compared with real flowers. Much depends on how faithfully you can follow the natural posture, curves, and rolls of flower petals. Worgan's book on the

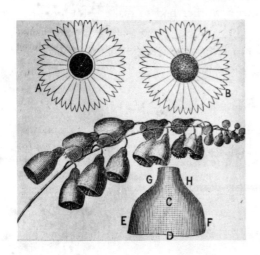

44. The simple mechanics of daisies and bluebells. (From Jones and Williams' *Making Household Elegancies*)

subject emphasizes the need for keeping a fresh flower before you for reference; it is very sound advice.

First, two flowers of the kind to be modeled were brought to the table and one was placed in a glass of water for preservation and reference. The other flower was dissected petal by petal and leaf by leaf. Each petal and each leaf as it was removed was placed on a piece of paper and the outline traced off with a sharp, soft pencil. The paper patterns were then laid on the wax sheets one by one, traced with a sharp pencil and then cut out with the scissors. This was followed by shaping.

Aside from the colored wax mentioned, the wax flower maker's kit must also have some iron, steel, or brass wire of various sizes (say, from 16 to 24 gauge) for stems and for binding, some colored tissue paper (this is colored green or brown, as the case may be, and is used to wrap around the wire stems), a small and a large pair of scissors, dry powder dyes for tinting, a small knife, a spirit lamp, and a set of tools used in forming petals and leaves.

At one time a full set of forming tools cost about $2.00 and such kits had as many as twenty pieces. Of course, if you have a metal cutting lathe in your workshop and really know how to use it, you can set several gadgets that will duplicate perfectly the orthodox article. These consist of small brass balls ranging in diameter from $\frac{1}{4}$ to $\frac{1}{2}$ inch mounted at the end of a $\frac{1}{8}$-inch brass rod. These are heated gently over the flame of a spirit or alcohol lamp and used to cup the flat petals of flowers like the rose or the tulip. The cupping is done by slight pressure from the warm brass ball while the petal is resting on a soft small pillow made by filling a small silk bag with talcum powder. If you have no lathe, you can use glass-

45. Some of the tools that comprised the kits of wax flower makers in the 1860's. (From Jones and Williams' *Making Household Elegancies*)

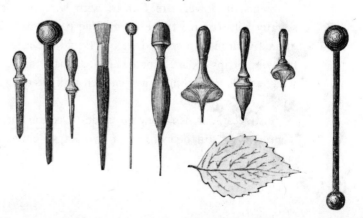

topped hat pins or any other device with a smooth, rounded body that will take and hold a bit of heat.

Stems of flowers are formed with wire of various gauges wrapped spirally with colored tissue paper. The paper may also be used white and dipped with molten colored wax or liquid dye after it has been applied to the wire. Strips about an inch wide are usually used. If the paper applied is white and is to be dipped into molten wax later, there is no need to apply adhesive of any kind.

Pistils and stamens may be made of cotton threads of different sizes. They may be stiffened in one of two ways—either by dipping them in a heavy solution of starch, or impregnating them with wax colored in the proper manner, although many are white in their natural state. In the case of the thread treated with starch, it will be necessary to supply oil colors in case anything except white is indicated.

Of all the flowers that may be used as models for reproduction in wax the rose is perhaps the most tempting. It is also among the most difficult to do, and the beginner is, therefore, advised to acquire some skill in making simpler flowers, especially when delicate tinting of pink or yellow is required. Less skill is needed with almost solid, deep reds. However, the rose offers still other demands on skill not easily acquired.

All of the instructors in wax flower making recommended that the worker make each part of a flower (or several sets of parts if more than one flower was to be modeled) and have these parts spread out before him when assembly was begun. In the case of the fuchsia (46) you not only outline each part needed but draw it to actual size. To start quickly, trace off these patterns and go to work. Assembly of such delicate flowers calls

XCI. A group of wax flowers with and without (opposite) the glass dome used to cover them. A bed was formed with lichen and sprig moss and a monarch butterfly was placed in the lily. This represents an almost-perfect specimen of the old craft.

for some patience. You should certainly be thoroughly relaxed and should work with good light.

Another little tool the authors found immensely useful was not mentioned in connection with the old kits for the simple reason that it did not exist: we refer to the little electrically-heated gadgets used for wood burning that come with pyrographic kits sold in toy departments. This can be used in welding one piece of wax to another in assembly. Previously, welding was accomplished in a much more difficult way by passing the parts to be joined over the flame of a spirit lamp. The pyrographic instrument should not be used at full heat, however. If you are not handy enough to place a rheostat in series with the device to cut down its heat, then you can heat it fully and remove it from the circuit until it has cooled sufficiently to permit softening of the wax rather than melting it on contact. Often in this work you can use little strips of properly colored wax to apply to such welds, much as you might apply solder in making a joint. The tool is especially useful for attaching leaves to wire stems, the stems always applied to the underside of the leaf where the ridge left by the wire will not be seen. Since the wire is underneath the leaf, you can run it almost full length to give a stronger joint. In such cases, the little strips of "soldering wax" may be effectively used in covering up the wire, the leaf being laid face down on the table while this operation is in progress.

Natural leaves are not perfectly flat. Therefore, after the stem is attached it is necessary to pass the leaf over an alcohol flame several times until it becomes pliable enough to respond to slight pressure from the fingertips to mold it into shape. Leaves curve gracefully downward due to gravity. The curving and forming are always done while the leaf rests on the soft talcum pad already mentioned.

If you find it difficult to heat the flower petals or leaves over the flame of a spirit lamp, then try a much more reliable but slower method: dip into hot water the wax object to be formed. Most waxes respond well if they are first subjected to a temperature of about 120°F.

Returning to the fuchsia, start from the bottom of the blossom. This may be set down as a general rule. It is also necessary in all cases of flower-making, as must be obvious even to a beginner, to start from the inside and work out.

The stem for the fuchsia should be made of No. 20 wire wrapped with tissue and colored, preferably by dipping it in green-tinted wax. This not only makes for well-protected tissue, but also forms a wax base which makes the fixture of the four calyx members simple. Attachment to the stem is achieved by warming one calyx member at a time and the wax paper-covered wire as well. The wax will have to be heated to a point just below melting. At this temperature it is rather puttylike, and the calyx members can be fastened to the wax on the paper-covered wire by firm pressure from your fingers. At the same time, the fingers mold the calyx members around the stem and weld them together to form what appears

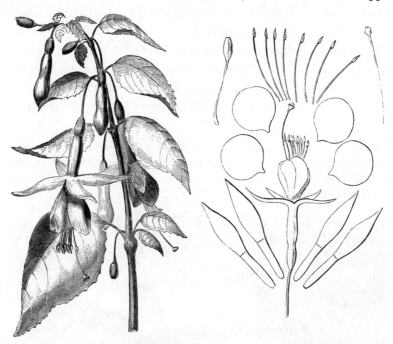

46. The fuchsia and its parts, actual size. (From *Making Wax Flowers*)

to be a solid cup at the base of the assembled calyx. The wire stem should extend about ½ inch above the bottom of the calyx. This will be found helpful in putting in the stamens, which are made of wax-impregnated thread. The tiny spearlike formation at the end of the stamen is of molten wax of appropriate color. The wax of the first dip is allowed time to congeal after removal before the second dip. This follows the technique of candle-dipping in Colonial times.

Inasmuch as the cluster of petals closes off the view of the bottom of the cup formed by them, you may take a few liberties in installing the stamens. Binding them with silk thread to the wire stem is quite permissible. It is easiest to weld each stamen to the end of the stem first, with a few drops of molten wax applied with a medicine dropper. Thus the stamens are anchored until you can bind them with thread.

This little pool of wax will also help in the installation and assembly of the petals, especially if you have a pyrographic pen. The tip of this may be pushed into the tiny pool of cold wax to remelt it, at which time the pointed base of each preformed petal is pushed into place and held with tweezers until the wax has congealed.

Thus, you may discover that this wax flower business is not as difficult as you had thought. But if you are a bit apprehensive about the prospect of the fuchsia, you may want to start with something still simpler. You may feel more comfortable with the ordinary daisy—our first venture,

XCII. How wax sheets are cut from a cake of wax by means of a warm, sharp knife. A sheet or sheets of Bristol board placed in the bottom of the tin box raises the level of the wax cake above the top edges of the box so that sheets of varying thickness may be shaved off the top of the cake.

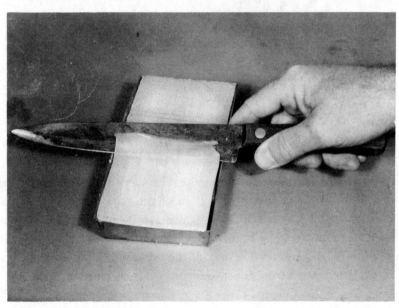

incidentally. As will be noted in illustration 45, the daisy should tax neither skill nor patience. The buttonlike wax center is easy to form and to attach to the stem, which is made exactly like the fuchsia stem but with No. 22 wire. The calyx is easily molded around the end of this wire and the deep brown buttonlike center of the daisy may be sprinkled with dry mustard powder after it has been smeared with a bit of dull varnish.

The petals are simply "welded" in beneath the buttonlike center. If the flowers are to be arranged so that the calyx is not to be seen, then there is no need of installing it. If it is to be seen, then the calyx may be installed after the petals are anchored.

A number of years ago when we made our first wax daisies and black-eyed Susans, we knew nothing about coloring wax with colors ground in oil or in japan. We discovered, however, that japan colors can be painted directly on wax surfaces; thus were our first crude little posies prepared. This is mentioned not by way of recommendation (coloring wax is very easy and colored wax is far more attractive), but simply to point out that in cases where touching-up is required or where streaks of color are needed on petals, japan colors can be applied successfully with a small brush. Colors ground in oil are much more difficult to handle on wax.

Few Victorian ladies mounted their wax flowers under glass domes or in shadow boxes without adding an authentic touch of nature in the form of dried leaves, grass, moss, lichen, or perhaps a butterfly poised on a flower. Both moss and lichen may be worked in around the bottom of a dome-enclosed bouquet to cover crudities left exposed.

Shadow boxes in which to mount your work may still be had at low cost in most antique shops, or your husband might make one in his cellar workshop. He can easily do this, especially if you desire a small oblong setting. All that is needed is a walnut picture frame of the type popular during the 1860's or '70's. A plush-, silk- or velvet-lined box about three inches deep is made from plywood and the old frame is fastened to the open top of this, as seen in 41. The glass is set tightly in the frame because of the destructive effect of dust. Many Victorian picture frames were thus converted by husbands, although every furniture shop carried a supply of shadow boxes in oval, round, oblong, square, or octagonal shapes.

Old glass domes with turned walnut bases are a little harder to find but, here and there, the antique shops offer them for $5 or less. If you cannot find a dome, don't despair; for they are still manufactured and may be obtained from the A-Bit Products Co., 4949 Sheldon Road, Chicago 40, Illinois.

XCIII. A small group of wax narcissus modeled in wax. This is an easy flower for beginners to work with.

Smithing, A Man's Hobby

{ 17 }

Many years ago, we had our first brush with smithing during a summer vacation in a small Vermont town. To while away the lazy, carefree hours, we visited the village smith, a huge, powerful man whose ancestry was the solid stock of the Green Mountain Boys. His father and his father's father had toiled over the same anvil and pumped the same bellows beneath the same great oak that spread its luxurious branches over the little forge which for nearly 150 years had supplied the townspeople with horseshoes, strap hinges, mending irons, foot-scrapers, and cranes for their hearths.

During slack hours this great, vigorous man took it upon himself to teach a city slicker some of the elements of his trade. Before that slicker had returned to New York, he could forge a bolt in the pritchel hole, bend a strap on the horn of the anvil, swage with a sledge, and cut with a hardie. And with it all came a certain sense of mastery that made iron and steel yield to mere flesh. Forging is a hardy hobby and can be real fun, as well as marvelous exercise.

Very well, you say, but where do I learn and where do I establish a forge and at what expense? To start with, you can learn the elements from simple instructions. Smithing has but few basic operations. A small forge may be established in a basement, the corner of a garage, or a shed. Cost can be moderate, especially if an alert novice watches for a country auction where a farm forge complete with tools and anvil is going on the block. We have seen these knocked down for as little as $10. Even new equipment need not place too much strain on the family budget. A man may have all he needs for less than a year's expense at his country club. For instance, a new pan-type forge complete with hand-operated blower costs between $25 and $35; $35 to $50 will buy an anvil; and a good set of tools need not exceed $40.

No matter what the type of forge, it will have to be connected to a chimney. For a cellar installation connections are simply made with the furnace flue or directly into the chimney itself.

The feet of the forge should be secured to the concrete floor with lag bolts. Otherwise, the forge will creep when the blower or blast fan is operated, unless one has an electrically-operated air supply.

You won't require a large, heavy anvil unless you plan to make wagon springs. One that weighs 75 to 100 pounds is adequate. It will have to be mounted on a large wooden block, as illustrated in 48. If the anvil is set up in a shed with a dirt floor, the wooden block may be cut longer and buried for a distance of two feet. The height of 30 inches shown may have to be increased or decreased a bit, depending on the size of the man. The 30-inch height is correct for a man about 5 feet 6 inches tall. The various hand tools required by a beginner are shown in 48, with the anvil.

The forge is used for heating iron that is to be worked on the anvil. It is also used for welding, hardening, and tempering.

Illustration 49 will give some idea of making a good forge fire. The smith of old was very particular about his fire. It had to be just right. A clean, compact fire, as free as possible from impurities, must be developed by the use of sulphur-free bituminous soft coal.

To start the fire, you must clean the pan and wad up a pile of newspaper in the center, surrounding this with small kindling and coal, banked around the edges of the pan, ready to be raked into place. You can speed up the process by operating the hand-cranked blower. Then, as the kindling reaches a high temperature and the paper is completely burned away, push some of the coal into the fire. As it ignites, push more and more into place until a cone of fire is produced, as shown in 49. It may be added that good blacksmiths are constantly fussing with their fires.

If you do not wish to "huff and puff" at the forge, here is the advice of an old-timer, as recalled by the authors. Once you have a good fire and know how to keep it, there is no need to finish a piece after its first heating. In short, breathless haste and continuous hammer blows that will exhaust you in a minute or two are unnecessary. The old-time smiths were a leisurely lot and worked with a certain rather slow rhythm. They had to in order to last out the day. After every few strokes, a smith relaxed his muscles by letting the hammer bounce or vibrate a few times on the anvil.

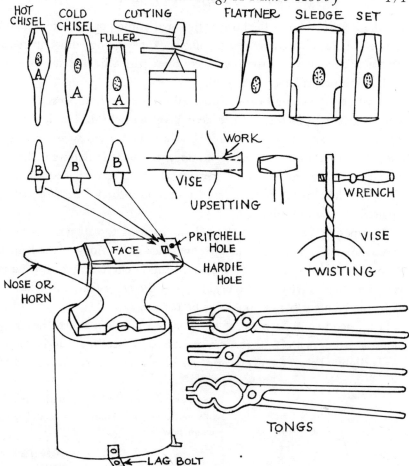

47. A standard anvil. When placed on the auction block at farm sales they often fail to bring a bid. New ones are inexpensive.

Thus he rested his arm and could complete a twelve-hour day. If this is not done, smithing will be an exhausting business.

Heated iron may be formed or shaped just so fast and no faster, no matter how much fury you put into it. Hot iron "flows" under the hammer and blows must be distributed evenly over the surface. By a careful distribution of blows, a good smith can make a bar of iron do almost anything; he may bend it gently, taper it, round it, cut it, or flatten it. But none of these operations is accomplished with a single heating.

White heat (incandescence) is unnecessary for a simple job of bending; the iron is laid over the nose of the anvil at the point where it is to be changed in shape. A cherry red is sufficient for bending, although reheating may be required. In forging a very thick bar, a light punch or chisel mark at the proper point is helpful.

If you are planning to forge iron railing for the front steps, you may want to give a ½-inch iron bar a decorative twist. In this work, only the center of the bar is heated, and this by laying the bar crosswise on the pan and piling coal around it. After heating, the piece is removed, the cold end is placed in a vise, and a monkey wrench is placed on the opposite cold end when the twisting begins. In all probability, several heatings will be required. (See illustration 49.)

In tapering (drawing, as the old smiths used to call it), the heated piece is placed over the horn of the anvil and drawn along as the hammer blows rain down on it. In this case, tapering is effected by a distribution of blows; more, that is, at the beginning of the taper than at the base. In short, the hammer blows, too, must be tapered.

To a good smith, a piece of hot iron is a plastic material; he can do almost anything with it. If, for instance, he has a piece of ½-inch iron rod that is slightly below the diameter needed for a job, he increases the diam-

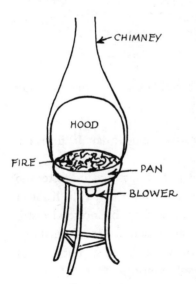

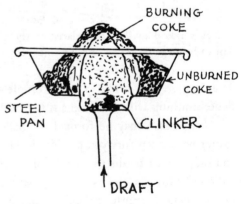

48. A small, pan-type forge with a hand-operated blower. These cost about $25 when new.

49. An expertly managed forge fire will be kept as illustrated here.

eter by a very simple operation he calls "upsetting." To do this he merely places the rod or bar in the fire, heats it to a high temperature, and then places the hot end on the anvil or in a vise in a vertical position, striking the cold end heavily with his hammer. This causes the hot end to mush out, or increase in diameter. A white heat is needed, as well as a big hammer and all you have in the way of blows.

If you have a few punches in your kit, there is no need to bore holes in an iron bar, for you can punch them. Heat the iron white hot, place it flat on the anvil, and strike it with the punch. This drives a hole about half-way through. Then turn the bar over on the anvil so that the half-punched hole will be directly over the pritchel hole. Put the punch in place again and strike. This should complete the operation.

To cut a flat bar use a chisel and red heat. If you have been fortunate in obtaining a complete set of smithy tools, you will find among them chisels provided with heavy metal tongues that will slip into the square hole in the anvil. Place the hot bar on the cutting edge of the chisel at the proper point and strike a few blows with a heavy hammer.

Any kind of a graceful curve in flat bar or square iron bar may be formed by working over the horn of the anvil and applying moderate heat frequently. The beginner's trouble here is that he wants to work too fast. The smith was a cautious, patient man, never in a hurry. Iron yields as iron —slowly.

It was one of the jobs of the local blacksmiths of colonial times to fabricate weathervanes from $\frac{1}{8}$-inch iron plate. A design was made by cutting the plate with small chisels, heating one section of the plate at a time, and by trimming the crude cuts with round or half-round files. The hinges were riveted in place.

In summing up smithing, we may say that much of the skill required is in keeping a forge fire properly, and in heating metal to the various temperatures needed for the various anvil operations. In some cases, high heat is required, in others only a cherry-red heat.

The composition of the metal being worked on is another factor. For wrought (soft) iron or mild steel, most work should be done at a temperature below welding heat, say, at about a light cherry-red. On the other hand, tool steel, which amateurs often work into small tools, should never be heated above a cherry-red because it will "burn," as the smith says.

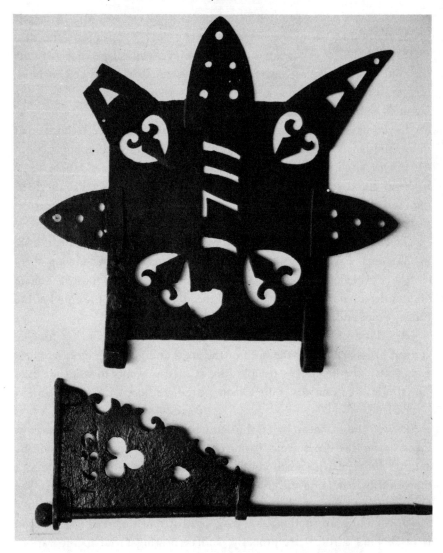

XCIV. Plate-type weathervanes from the latter 17th and early 18th century. The one at the right, made in 1711, once graced the roof of North Church at Danvers, Massachusetts. The other was made in 1682. Note that unlike later vanes, these do not have arrows; rather, the whole plate moves. (*Courtesy Essex Institute, Salem, Massachusetts*)

When it burns it becomes scrap, having become too brittle for practical purposes.

Heat should be distributed uniformly throughout a piece of metal. This is rather difficult at times. For instance, the thin sections of a piece may become incandescent before the inside reaches color. The smith remedies this situation by immersing the piece in an oil bath after heating. The thin sections of the metal that have reached incandescence will be cooled immediately by this immersion, while the heat in the thick sections of the metal will not be greatly lowered.

Most cutting of metals on the anvil can be done at cherry-red or below. Tapering or upsetting can also be done at this color when you are working with wrought iron. Slightly higher temperatures are required with steel. Most twisting can be done with cherry-red heat, as well as bending on the anvil, either over the edge (abruptly) or over the horn.

For the beginner, welding is perhaps the most difficult job. Hence, he is advised to try a few test pieces before attempting to handle a real job. Get such pieces at any metal supply house and practice welding with a few feet of ½-inch wrought-iron bar for only a few cents a foot.

For welding, the smith wants what he calls a "reducing fire." This means a large fire filling most of the pan and only moderately hot—high red in place of white heat. The blower is used only moderately.

One of the secrets of welding is to heat the metal slowly so that it will be heated uniformly throughout. This long exposure to the fire means the formation of hard scale on the surfaces of the pieces to be welded. The scale may be removed by pouring powdered borax over the metal while it is hot. Thereafter, heating is continued until the surface of the metal becomes "sticky"; in short, until it shows signs of melting. This temperature is easily recognized because tiny sparks begin to fly from the surface of metal that is hot enough to weld.

When this heat is reached, the worker takes one of the pieces to be welded (naturally both are heated together), places it on the face of the anvil, and strikes several sharp blows to remove dross and scale. This operation is repeated with the second piece while the first lies on the anvil. Then the heated portions are placed, with the aid of tongs, one over the other in a proper position, and a few relatively light blows are struck at the point of the proposed weld. If the metal shows signs of "sticking," real muscle is brought into play. If you do not have your weld then, you must repeat the whole operation.

Some years ago, we were hard-pressed to duplicate a hand-wrought iron hinge on the cover of a very old pine chest we had purchased. Black-

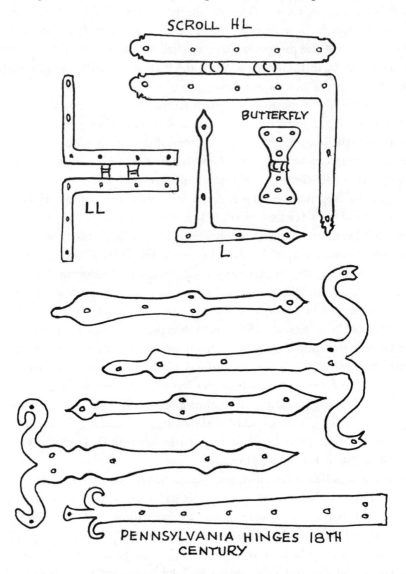

50. Outlines of some iron hinges of the kind used during the 18th century.

XCV. An antique hinge simulated in lead, the surface of which is treated with the peen end of a ball peen hammer and then painted a dull black.

smiths being scarce, and custom work of this kind very expensive, we decided to try working in another medium—lead. We took the old hinge off, traced its outline on lead sheet, and cut it out with tinner's snips. After trimming the edges with a jackknife and a file, we laid the piece on a hard board and went over its surface carefully with the peen end of a ball peen hammer. The result was an almost perfect duplicate of the hand-forged iron hinge. We mention this trick for the cheaters who may have no appetite for the hardy business of smithing but who still have an occasional job to be done.

Needless to say, simulated hinges made from lead are given a coat of dull black paint for finish. In case some of our antique-minded friends want to use this method, we are including a drawing (50) of some old-time hardware designs, all authentic.

Many useful and attractive items for home exteriors and interiors can be fashioned in the smithy's shop: wrought-iron foot scrapers, strap hinges, chimney figures, weather vanes, door latches, fireplace cranes, andirons, trivets, and certainly more. The next time you visit an Early American house, look closely at the iron accessories around and about—you'll be sure to come home brimming with ideas for your own house and for invigorating hours with your forge and anvil.

Old-Time Pewter in the Modern Manner

{ 18 }

Pewter was a craft metal in Japan and China at the beginning of the Christian era. For nearly two thousand years this soft, lustrous alloy of lead, tin, copper, and antimony has been in the service of the housewife. Up until the 1830's, America had its busy guild of pewterers who supplied all manner of utensils to those who could not afford silver. The final blow to the grand old trade came when American potteries took vigorous root in the fertile soil of American enterprise. Grandma would have no more of pewter; her heart was won by the glitter of flint glass, the gay decorations of painted tinware and china.

But pewter as an alloy has survived and is still produced in a form suitable for craftsmen and hobbyists. Well-stocked craft stores carry this metal alloy in disks and squares of various sizes and gauges. If your local dealer does not stock it, you may order it from Fellowcrafters, Inc., 64 Stanhope Street, Boston, Mass., or from Handcraft Supplies, Springfield, Mass. It is a relatively inexpensive metal.

The kit of tools needed to work pewter is modest enough. Thick sheets must be cut with a fine-tooth coping saw, thin ones with a pair of tinner's snips. You will also need a bundle of 4-0 steel wool, a small light ball peen hammer, a few fine files, a vise with an anvil and a horn, and some wooden molds that may be turned by a friend with a wood-turning lathe. If you wish to etch pewter, and most workers do, add a small bottle of nitric acid and a pint of asphaltum paint to the list. An old-fashioned flatiron, held bottomside up in a rack, makes an excellent surface upon which to work.

In case you succumb completely to the hobby and wish to work extensively with it, it is possible that you will want to buy special anvils,

178

hammers, snips, mallets, and a set of six forming stakes which may be held in a vise, over which pewter is held during the forming process. A special tapered mandrel for curving pewter is available in steel. However, the beginner may use either the horn or a vise anvil or a short length of two-inch cold roll steel held in a vise for this purpose.

If sheet pewter is too thick to be cut with snips, then it will have to be held in a vise and cut with a jeweler's fine-toothed saw. To prevent chattering, and to give a cleaner edge, it is best to place the sheet material over a $\frac{1}{8}$-inch piece of plywood before the metal is placed in the vise. You then saw through the plywood and the sheet metal simultaneously.

The amateur pewterer will do well to curb his ambitions until he gains some experience in handling the metal—specifically, in working up flat pieces. These may be etched according to instructions in this chapter, or the design may be fret-sawed.

Interesting and useful articles can be made by sawing: pewter monograms for pocketbooks, buckles, insignia for wooden book-ends or for wooden wall plaques. Sheet pewter in various thicknesses comes ready for application. Usually a thickness of about $\frac{1}{16}$ inch is suitable for work of this sort.

Let us assume you are going to saw out a monogram for your wife's handbag. Unless you are better than most, you will sketch a number of suggestions on paper until you come up with the one that satisfies you. This design may then be transferred to the pewter surface as follows:

First, the surface of the sheet metal must be clean. To remove completely the last trace of grease left by the rolling mill, rub the surface gently in one direction with fine steel wool. Then lay a piece of fresh carbon paper over the metal and place the paper design over this. If you go over the design with a sharp, hard pencil, it transfers to the paper. However, some alloys of pewter (there are many) make such transfer difficult, due to their composition. In that case, you may have to paint the surface of the pewter with Chinese white (show-card paint). After this is dry, draw the design or monogram over it with a sharp pencil. Later, the Chinese white can easily be washed away with warm water.

Some amateur pewterers use different saw blades for sheet pewter of different thicknesses. This is quite unnecessary. Pewter is a very soft metal, easily cut. Speed in sawing will not be greatly increased by using a coarse saw, and the coarser the saw, the rougher the cut edges. It is best to use the finest jeweler's saw blade that can be found. The fine saw will cut fast enough and leaves a nice edge that needs only a little trimming with a fine file.

In producing fretwork in pewter, you must guard against two things: since pewter is a soft metal, you will be apt to make scratches and digs. The vise in which the work is held while being sawed may produce ugly surface marks unless the jaws of the vise are covered with soft wood. Some craftsmen cut two small wooden blocks and wire them temporarily to the jaws of the vise.

Pewter bends easily. Remember this while you are making the saw cuts. The bending problem can be solved if you back up the sheet pewter with a thin piece of plywood while it is being held in the vise. You can easily cut through the pewter and the wood simultaneously.

The presence of the wood also tends to eliminate chatter while you saw. In any event, see to it that the work is moved repeatedly in the vise so that the cutting is kept as close to the vise jaws as possible. This prevents vibration or chatter and makes for a clean edge.

In pewter fretwork as in wood fretwork, it is necessary to drill a hole or holes (depending upon design) in the pewter—wood, too, if that is used— so that the saw blade may be threaded through to start cutting. Perfection in fretwork is attained by following the design lines closely and finishing the raw sawed edges of the pewter. (You will want to remove all evidence that your monogram was cut with a saw.) You must place the work back in the vise and, with a fine needle file, remove all the burrs and trim the

51. How to begin the forming of a pewter bracelet. Here many light blows from the hammer will be much more satisfactory than a few heavy ones.

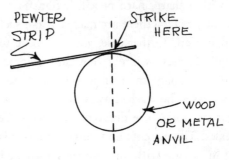

PEWTER STRIP   STRIKE HERE

WOOD OR METAL ANVIL

edges. Follow with an application of fine garnet or emery cloth. The really meticulous worker goes still further; he rubs the article, sawed surfaces and all, with a rag carrying carborundum valve grinding compound, which is superfine abrasive dust in oil. In treating the outer surface of pewter with this, move the rag back and forth in one direction only. A beautiful, silvery gray surface results. The surface may be preserved indefinitely by the application of clear lacquer or plastic covering.

Sooner or later most beginners in pewtercraft, fascinated by the medium, want to try their skill at forming the metal into shallow and then deep dishes. This may sound difficult, but it really isn't. Remember that pewter is the most malleable alloy; it responds well to mallet blows and, if you are patient, there is no reason why you can't be successful in your first attempts.

The one basic rule in forming pewter with mallets and hammers is to use many light blows rather than a few heavy ones. Many beginners wield one heavy blow where they should use twenty light ones.

Sheet pewter is "dished out" or made into bowls by the combined use of wooden forms and metal stakes, as illustrated in 52. (Sheet pewter of No. 16 gauge is best for this purpose.) Both the stakes and the forms are in hobby shops handling sheet pewter. The wooden forms are turned on a lathe and are usually of rock maple. If the hobbyist has a small wood-turning lathe, he can make his own forming blocks.

In forming deep bowls, a series of several blocks has to be used. Hobby supply shops sell such combinations—each block a little deeper than the preceding one—adjusted to the shrinkage that takes place as the sheet pewter is worked on.

The beginner should avoid making pewter bowls with deep (say 1½- to 3-inch) draws requiring a series of blocks and careful working over several types of stakes. Instead, he should make his first bowls with draws of not more than one inch—ashtrays, for instance. A draw may be done on a single block and may be used many times. It comes for less than a dollar at an art-supply shop.

The preliminary step in making an ashtray is illustrated in 52. No. 16 gauge sheet pewter can be cut with ordinary snips. The disk should be about the size indicated in the drawing. Begin by placing the disk over the hollow section of the forming block, holding it there with one hand, and

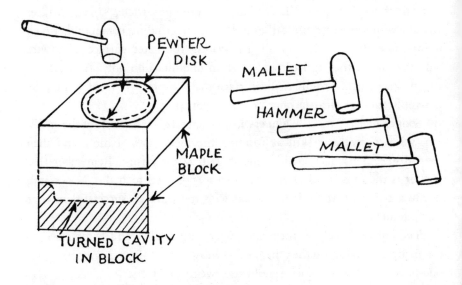

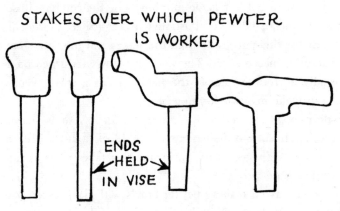

52. Forming blocks are made of maple or other hard wood with depressions turned on a lathe. Pewter discs are dished out and formed by laying them over the depressions and carefully hammering the discs into the depressions.

striking it with a wooden mallet. Note that the ashtray to be made has no rim, the most practical kind for beginners.

What you must do is to force the sheet of pewter gradually down into the depression by a series of mallet blows until it finally conforms to the depression in the block. The round end of the wooden mallet is for striking. See that your blows are just hard enough to make the metal yield slightly at each strike. Before you make the first strike (52) be sure that the disk of pewter is placed concentrically over the circular depression in the wood. This precaution must be taken until the sheet pewter is dished out enough to fit partially into the depression.

After you strike the first blow, strike another next to it and continue around the edge of the disk at a point just above the edge of the depression in the block. Twenty to twenty-five trips around the disk with the mallet may be necessary before the piece begins to shape up.

When it does take shape, you will no doubt be rather discouraged. The edge of the pewter dish that overlaps the lip of the depression in the bowl will begin to wrinkle or "ruffle." This is unavoidable. Thus pewterers, either amateur or professional, must take time out to correct these ruffles as they form.

In the case of the simple ashtray, ruffles may be removed by using the flat face of the mallet around the edges of the tray—without removing it. If kinks form deeper within the tray, it is necessary to remove the work from the wooden form and to hammer out the wrinkles and ruffles in the simple manner illustrated in 51. It is shown here that this is done by inverting the tray, holding it over one of the metal stakes, and hammering out the kinks and imperfections. It may be necessary to make several trips to the stakes before the job is finished.

Some prefer to change from a wooden mallet to a small ball peen hammer when working out the dimples and imperfections in the nearly finished tray. Of course you will want to have a perfectly flat bottom in the dish. Place the finished article on a flat metal surface (an old-fashioned flatiron held upside down in a vise, for instance) and strike the bottom repeatedly with the flat face of a wooden mallet. You finish the piece completely by filing the rough edges of the rim and going over them with fine emery. Then rub the whole surface, inside and out, with steel wool.

In case you wish to use the sheet pewter for a square box or other article requiring right-angle bends, the little device shown in illustration 24, Chapter 11, will be helpful.

If you keep on working with pewter you will, sooner or later, want to solder the metal. This can be dangerous because pewter is an alloy with a low melting point. You will need a small piece of asbestos board on which to place the work and a small alcohol blowtorch operated by a rubber tube to the mouth. After the two edges of pewter to be joined are placed together in the proper position (if they can be held by clamps or weights, so much the better), the sections are covered with what is known as pewter flux, obtainable at your craftsman shop. The affected parts of the metal should be made scrupulously clean with steel wool before the flux is applied.

The solder used is of the ordinary wire type without a flux core—in short, plain solder. It is cut into short lengths about ¼ inch long. These are laid almost, but not quite, end to end along the joint to be soldered. The flame from the torch is then applied and is permitted to sweep over the joint first in one direction and then in the opposite direction until the solder melts and flows. *Never let the flame remain in one position too long lest the pewter melt first.*

Bracelets, either etched or scrolled, may be easily made of sheet pewter No. 16 gauge. Following are the necessary information and directions for making a simple etched bracelet.

Etching pewter with acid leaves a mat finish without luster, in contrast to the silvery, lustrous surface of the unetched metal. The theory behind etching is simple. Certain paints are not affected by the acids that attack pewter. Therefore, you may cover pewter with such paints, leaving the drawing or design bare. Thus, when the pewter is exposed to the acid for a few minutes, the exposed metal is etched while the part covered with the paint remains untouched. The paint may then be dissolved. Asphaltum paint is used because it is easily removed after the etching is done. Initials and other designs can be applied according to these directions.

If you wish to take a design from a book or magazine, it is simple to apply it to pewter. Merely transfer the design to onionskin or tracing paper, place a piece of carbon paper beneath it, and trace onto the pewter. The asphaltum paint is applied as the design calls for.

In the case of the bracelet, however, it is perhaps best to form the article before the actual etching is done. It will be more convenient to scratch in the initials when the metal shape is lying flat. The asphaltum paint can be applied easily enough after the forming is done. The pewter strip will have to be held over a metal mandrel gripped firmly in a vise or over the horn of an anvil. First, place only the tip of the strip over the mandrel or horn, as illustrated in 51. Strike gently at the point indicated, and as the metal responds move the strip along, always remembering that pewter is formed not quickly by heavy blows, but slowly by many very light blows.

XCVI. Etching initials on a home-made pewter bracelet with acid. After the outline of the initials is scratched in, all but this area is covered with asphaltum paint which is left unaffected by the acid. The paint is easily removed with turpentine after the etching has been completed.

You should not attempt to give the bracelet its full curvature all at once. First give it a slight arc and repeat the process until the proper curvature is achieved. Then you will be ready to lay on the asphaltum paint—called a "resist" in the etching trade. A resist is a substance which is not affected by a strong acid-etching solution such as the three-parts water and one-part nitric acid which you will be using. Make just enough solution to cover the bracelet when it is immersed.

The degree to which etching is carried out depends on the worker; it can be deep or light. With a deep etching, pitting is apt to develop. Good etching is usually moderately light in character—just deep enough to produce a mat surface that will contrast well with the natural finish. To achieve this result, dip and remove your work repeatedly for examination until you have the proper depth of etching. Then wash it immediately in clean, running water to arrest further progress of the acid.

Many workers use adhesive tape for suspension during etching. With the bracelet you should simply attach the tape to the back and dip it, pulling it out of the solution every few minutes to examine the surface.

You can easily remove the asphalt paint by applying turpentine or other solvent. While you are in the process of etching, don't forget that nitric acid is dangerously corrosive and may cause painful burns on the skin unless it is quickly neutralized. Therefore, as a precautionary measure, you should have a saturated solution of bicarbonate of soda at hand.

A New Look for Old China & Glassware

{ 19 }

Many years ago F. Stanhope Hill, a Bostonian, spent a long time in Germany studying porcelain painting under mastercraftsmen Franz Till of Dresden and G. F. Deininger of Munich. August Klinke's standard work on the subject, *Anleitung Zum Malen auf Porzellan,* was Mr. Hill's Bible. Returning to this country, Hill was so full of enthusiasm for porcelain painting as a hobby that he itched to do something about it. His little book, *Porcelain Painting After The Dresden Manner,* is among the rarest of the old-time craft books in our collection.

We are not so naïve as to propose that the work of Hill, Deininger, or even that of Mary Jones in the 1860's, can be duplicated. Indeed, were it not for the fact that easily applied colors can now be purchased for the decoration of porcelain and glass, this chapter would not be included.

J. Marsching and Company of New York sold Royal Dresden China Colors for amateur use back in the 1850's, but these were vitrifiable preparations that had to be carefully and expertly fired in kilns after being applied. At present, it is possible to purchase paints which, after they are applied to porcelain or glass, may be fired in a short time in the kitchen oven. Although not to be compared with the old-time craft, this version offers promise to those of us who have hankered for a chance at artistic expression, for much can be done with it. You may paint little pieces for gifts or for the house, using plain white china plates and cups picked up in the second-hand stores.

While some expert craftsmen who decorate china prefer to grind and mix their own colors, this technique is not for the beginner. It is slow and tricky, and years of experience are required to master it. Better by far to use ready-made preparations. These ready-to-apply colors may be found in

187

small amounts at most of the large hobby shops dealing in ceramic supplies. They are applied with ordinary brushes, as in oil painting. After application, however, they must be placed in a ceramic kiln and fired because they are vitreous materials. During firing they flux or melt and thereby become firmly attached to the china or pottery on which they have been painted. Thereafter they will bear up as well as the decoration on regular store china.

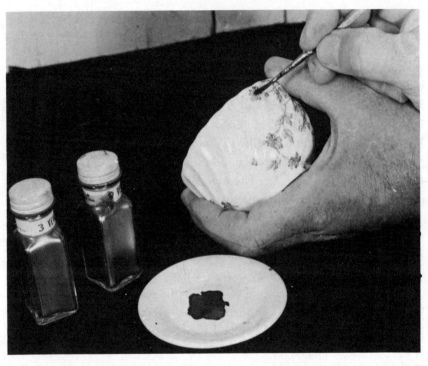

XCVII. Plain white china cups and saucers purchased inexpensively at second-hand stores can be painted for gifts or household use.

Because a rather expensive kiln must be used to apply heat to this china over a relatively long period of time, you will have to search out the owner of such a kiln in your own or a nearby neighborhood. The ceramic hobby is so popular today that this should not be difficult. Every town of any size has hobbyists, and practically all large cities have supply shops or schools equipped with kilns through which articles may be processed at little cost.

For those who do not want to use the vitrifiable colors because of the need to kiln-fire them, there is another way out. During the past few years several types of paint for coloring china, pottery, and glass have been developed and are now available either directly from the manufacturer or from hobby shops. The manufacturers of these materials do not maintain that they are as good as the kiln-fired colors but they do assert, and rightly, that they are the next best thing. They set extremely hard and may be washed hundreds of times.

Among the new paints available for china, glassware, or metal is Dek-All, manufactured by the American Crayon Company of Sandusky, Ohio. Most large art stores carry these inexpensive materials which we may use to transform unadorned china, tumblers, or jugs into decorative pieces of lasting use. These paints, which come in a wide range of colors, are applied

XCVIII. Glasses decorated with the porcelainlike paints prepared especially for china and glassware. These paints endure a half-century of ordinary wear. (*Courtesy American Crayon Co.*)

with a small brush. The basic colors and the black and white supplied may be used for mixing any shade the worker wishes. The rules are the same as those for mixing oil- or water-colors. Transparent or semitransparent effects may result from light application, and opaque effects with two or more applications.

When the painting is done, the pieces are set in a cold kitchen oven, gas or electric. The oven is then turned on and allowed to heat to 300° F. and to remain there for fifteen minutes. After the heat is turned off, the articles are not removed until the oven has thoroughly cooled, with the door closed. This will take several hours.

Few of us are artists enough to paint in original designs without some help. The amateur may choose his design either from a book on antique china or on American or other folk art. Designs may be drawn on tracing paper and then traced onto the article itself, using ordinary carbon paper.

If you feel sufficiently capable, you may want to draw your own garland of flowers on your white china and paint it in. Do this with one of the special pencils now manufactured for writing on glass or glazed surfaces.

Not all of us can take a brush in hand and paint a picture or even a flower. This is actually a combination of drawing and painting. The old masters did it, but all of the amateurs working in the Dresden manner during the 1860's and 1870's first selected their subject, drew and redrew it on paper until they were satisfied with it, and then traced it on the surface of the porcelain to be painted with a special tracing paper sold in the art shops of the day. However, we have found that such special tracing paper is not at all necessary. Ordinary carbon paper for typewriters is quite adequate.

But first you must select and draw your design. You will save yourself disappointment if you are not too ambitious. Simple subjects such as fruit or a group of flowers are fine to start with. Unless you are far more talented than the average hobbyist, you will want to avoid the eighteenth-century figures and court scenes typical of the true Dresden.

The design, floral or fruit, should be drawn as carefully as possible on thin but tough draftman's tracing paper. Since this is translucent, you may be fortunate enough to find a picture or design of the correct size in a book or magazine. If you do, you can make a direct pencil tracing. Transferring this to the china plate is a very simple matter. Merely place a piece of carbon paper on the plate and put the tracing over it. Then go over the tracing on the paper firmly with a sharp pencil. It will leave an outline of the design or picture on the china.

XCIX. Pottery and tiles painted with the new materials that require only a brief low-temperature firing in the kitchen oven. (*Courtesy American Crayon Co.*)

Pottery: A Pastime for All Time

{ 20 }

During the late 1860's, Professor F. Schliemann, the German archeologist, unearthed many fragments of pottery on the site of ancient Troy. As a result of his research and publications, interest in the decorative arts of the Greeks, the Romans, the Egyptians, and the Carthaginians was revived. The S. W. Tilton Company of Boston, then one of the country's chief depots for the distribution of hobby materials, was quick to exploit this interest, especially among the young ladies of leisure who sought an outlet for their often considerable talents. By special arrangement with the professor, the Tilton company began to manufacture what was called Albert Ware in numerous classical shapes of unglazed pottery suitable for home decoration. Their catalog listed over 130 different forms ranging from the famous Portland Vase and Etruscan mugs to flasks from the Cesnola collection. However, it was not until specimens of the new craft were shown at the Philadelphia Centennial that the ladies of the Victorian era took up the idea and made it a fad that lasted until the early 1880's. One is still apt to come across an occasional piece in the few remaining attics holding treasures of that epoch: an Etruscan pitcher or possibly a section of a Greek column with a gilded capital intended for an umbrella stand, perhaps made by a student at Cooper Union in New York or the Cincinnati School of Design or in a class at Horticultural Hall in Boston.

Many years have passed since the popular Albert Ware was made. But anyone having the urge to engage in this fascinating pastime need not be discouraged. Between 1800 and 1915 millions of pieces of crockery were made in America in a multitude of shapes, and many with hints of classical form. Classical or not, all of this ware, although glazed for waterproofing, may quickly be given a suitable surface for classical or modern designs. If

192

small-town second-hand shops or antique dealers do not have a supply of this sturdy old ware, the country auctions offer specimens very reasonably. They range in size from the one-gallon pickle crock to the giant jug. Many of the old crocks and jugs were buff in color, suitable for decoration in vivid colors and Pennsylvania Dutch motifs.

C. Such old and inexpensive crockery, after being painted white and then decorated and varnished, may be used to enliven a room of almost any period.

First comes a thorough washing with warm water and soap followed by rinsing. Surface transformation from glaze to soft mat to take pencil, ink, or paint is quickly effected either by two coats of flat white paint or one of the waterproofing cement mixtures such as Medusa. Should you wish to avoid pure white for a background, you may tint flat white paints with any shade desired by adding color ground in oil. The scope of such work is wide enough to suit any taste and the inclusion of any classical note. For instance, while flat black instead of white cannot be used, a silhouette form of decoration may be rendered in white. On the other hand, if the background is flat white or tinted, you may use jet black or almost any color

CI. Painting in a design on an old piece of crockery that has been covered with white flat paint.

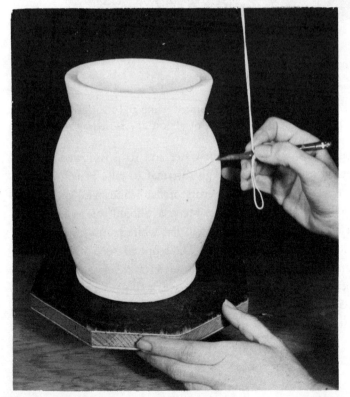

CII. Lines and bands may be traced on the sides of crocks and jugs by placing them on a turntable and using a pencil suspended from above on a string.

for the design. Much depends upon your sense of color value and contrast. There is now available waterproofing paint for cement in a fairly wide array of colors.

Coloring mediums may be oil, tempera, japan, or even Higgins colored inks. Higgins India ink on white or tinted surfaces is very effective, especially in the execution of classical Greek motifs. If colored Higgins inks are used, however, it may be necessary to paint over the designs twice to avoid the transparency of such mediums.

If you do not feel up to outlining your designs on the pottery freehand with a soft pencil, you have a safe way out. Even painting in bands is made delightfully easy by the use of the simple gadget illustrated. You can make such a contraption in an hour or so.

As for the form your designs take, there is no need to cling to classical devices or motifs. A vast field is open. Although the Pennsylvania Dutch did not decorate their pottery in the gay manner they used for their dower chests or brides' boxes, you may do so, and get fascinating results. The same holds for provincial Scandinavian, even Navaho or Aztec. Or if you feel bound to geometric forms because of limited talent, you need only use a compass, a ruler, and a French curve on a piece of paper. But how, you may ask anxiously, am I going to draw a design for circular application that will be so divided that it will come out correctly when applied? That, too, is simple.

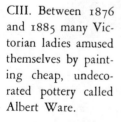

CIII. Between 1876 and 1885 many Victorian ladies amused themselves by painting cheap, undecorated pottery called Albert Ware.

First, take a band of paper of whatever width needed and run it around your jug, crock, or whatever your piece may be. Then cut off the excess of overlap with scissors and butt the ends accurately. Before you remove the paper band, carefully trace its exact position on the jug, pot, or crock with a soft lead pencil. This is particularly necessary where there is a tapering diameter.

Next, remove the paper and place it on a drawing board where you may draw in whatever design you have in mind. Then cut strips of carbon paper to the same width as the paper band and paste, carbon side out, to the back of the paper band bearing your drawing. Replace the band around the jug and hold it in place with a bit of rubber cement; you may then trace the design onto the pottery with a sharp pencil.

Even if you have irregular, round, or bellied surfaces in the work, mechanical assistance is possible in inking or painting in the design. Where Higgins India ink is used in geometric design on pure flat white—a delightful combination, incidentally, due to the high contrast—you may get real assistance with a flexible ruler or straightedge by bending a strip of

CIV (opposite) and **CV**. Designs from Tilton's *Decorating Pottery*, issued 1876.

celluloid to conform to the contour and using it with a lettering pen of proper width. Guarantee accuracy by drawing in outlines this way and later filling in with brush and Higgins India ink.

CVI. A suggestion for crockery decoration in the classical manner as illustrated in *Decorating Pottery*.

CVII. Motifs for pottery design from S. W. Tilton's *Decorating Pottery*.

The only awkward area on jugs is the shoulder or hip where curvature is extreme. What has been said above simply will not apply to this area. Here it must be freehand or nothing at all.

If you desire Pennsylvania Dutch or Scandinavian Provincial motifs on jugs and crocks, transferring with carbon paper in the manner described is quite in order. This provides the opportunity of making a satisfactory drawing before transferring it to the surface to be painted. For suitable paints and colors, see the reference to Dek-All in Chapter 19.

After your painting has been allowed to dry for forty-eight hours, give the piece a coat of water-white or spar varnish to preserve it.

CVIII. Painting an old crock with one of the new preparations that, as they dry hard and permanent, requires no firing.

Whistle As You Whittle

{ 21 }

When Levi Cushing's shop at 79 Broad Street, Boston, was producing the best of the carved figureheads for American sailing vessels during the early years of the nineteenth century, both woodcarving and whittling were at their height. Cushing was but one of hundreds of professional carvers; ordinary whittlers were legion—felons in their cells, sailors at leisure, farmers by their firesides, loafers at the village stores. It was both a grand old craft and a rewarding pastime.

Only two tools are needed for whittling—a knife, and a whetstone to keep its edge sharp. America's sculptors in wood produced millions of gaily decorated pieces that took a multitude of forms: toys for the children, decoys for hunters, signs for tavernkeepers, grotesque figures for the carousel, weathervanes, trade signs, and pieces for the mantel such as ships in bottles. Precious, indeed, are the relics from this era of the American whittler. Specimens of this folk art which remain bring staggering prices. And today many craftsmen are interested in the rudiments of the craft itself. They want especially to whittle quaint little creatures and models of their own and to decorate them brightly in the old-time manner.

Only the soft woods should be used. In the early days, white pine was a favorite medium, although poplar and basswood were also used. Hardwood or the semi-hardwoods such as mahogany or walnut are for the carver's chisel rather than for the whittler's blade. While the texture of balsa wood is not conducive to smooth, well-finished surfaces, this wood is easily cut, and beginners may gain sculpturing experience with it. Soft as it is, however, it requires the keenest sort of cutting edge, especially across grain. Wood with basically weak fiber is torn easily, rather than cut.

The difficulties in carving balsa wood may be overcome almost entirely by the diligent use of fine sandpaper, steel wool, and shellac after the carving or whittling has been done. Several coats of shellac (no thinning required) will help to build up a surface suitable for covering with bright and varicolored enamels. Balsa in block form may be found in any model supply shop.

Among other woods suitable for carving are red cedar, whitewood or yellow poplar, red gum, and really soft mahogany. Perhaps as you grow more proficient in the work you may wish to try your luck with some of the harder woods.

CIX. The sailing ship provided a tempting subject for whittlers since the days of yore. This was done by one of the authors years ago when he was not busy writing books like this.

In choosing a good whittling knife, throw caution to the winds as far as expense goes. Yes, you may whittle with a jackknife if you wish, but there is always the hazard of a blade that may close and catch a finger with it. Better by far buy a high-grade knife made for whittling. It is known to the trade as a sloyd knife, is inexpensive, and includes a small sharpening stone on which to dress the edge of the blade repeatedly.

As in woodcarving with chisels, the one great difference between a skilled professional and an impatient amateur is that the careful worker dresses the edges of his tools again and again while the novice does so only when the tools lose their cutting edge almost completely. So it is with the craftsman and the rank beginner in whittling. Even on the softest woods, the edge of the knife should be dressed after each few minutes of work.

You may possibly remember some of the instructions about using a plane in your first shop class in high school when you were taught to cut *with the grain*. The same rule holds in whittling. If you fail to follow it, difficulties will increase. For one thing, cutting will be harder and the danger of splitting off a piece will be greater.

Another thing, you will have to learn to do something which you were taught not to do when your Uncle Henry or your Aunt Minnie gave you your first jackknife: you were warned *never* to cut toward yourself, that is, with the knife blade aimed toward your stomach. Sometimes this rule must be set aside. But with care and patience there need not be any danger. Above all, you must learn to keep the hand that holds your work protected from a slip of the knife. If, as a beginner, you are afraid of an accident, cover your holding hand with a thick canvas or leather glove.

It should be noted that not all whittlers use the knife exclusively. In our chapter dealing with printing fabrics we show a set of small carving chisels. The use of such tools is certainly not against the rules. Many whittling jobs call for deep cuts perpendicular to the surface; in such cases the chisel is much more efficient than the knife.

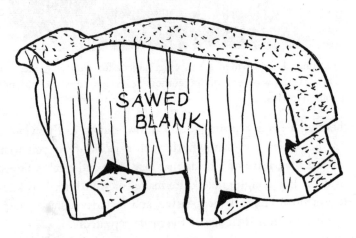

53. The form of a pig is roughed out on a band saw or with a coping saw before the whittling is begun.

Also, the modern worker may take advantage of a power tool which saves much labor. We refer to the power jigsaw with which a figure, whatever it may be, can be roughed out in the manner shown in 53. Such a simple beginning saves a lot of cutting. Naturally, the outline is first sketched on the wood.

54. Forms are sketched out on cross-section paper before transferring to wood.

The careful worker without natural skill in sculpture usually goes far beyond this in laying out his work and in planning the method of his whittling in any job. Using cross-section paper and drawing to scale, he makes several drawings of the type illustrated in 54. Such drawings offer invaluable assistance and should be available for constant reference.

After the jigsawed blank is made, you must whittle away large portions of excess wood, using sure, deep cuts to rough out the piece with a knife. This done, set about cutting in the detail. The ease with which this is accomplished may surprise you. Indeed, unless you are completely without talent, the whole operation will be simple and delightfully relaxing. Chances are that you will be immensely pleased even with your first efforts.

While some workers prefer to use only the jackknife in their work, foregoing even the roughing-out on the jigsaw, those who do not wish to

CX. An American eagle whittled from pine back in the time when he was a proud and ugly old bird.

martyr themselves unduly to authentic procedure may want to smooth the surface of the completely cut figure with a small file before the sandpaper and steel wool are used.

Of course, not all old-time whittling and carving was so finished. Some of it, as in the case of the American eagle shown in CX, was left with a rough surface. We still have amateur woodcarvers who persist in this method, feeling that it provides their cuttings with a quaint note. This is a matter of personal opinion.

Whittlers of the first half of the nineteenth century invariably used the gaudiest of colors with which to decorate their handcraft. This was a form of folk art, and folk art in any form never shied away from spectacular effects. Hence, we should have no fear of the gaily colored enamels in the chain stores. However, if you want the last ounce of glitter, you must cover the whittled model, whether an 1820 canal boat or an American eagle, with several coats of shellac, treating each coat with the finest steel wool. These preserve the high gloss of the enamel and make the colors strong enough to be worthy of their historical predecessors. If such colors are placed directly upon untreated wood, several coats will be necessary because much of the first one will be absorbed.

There can be little doubt of your success in whittling if you start with modest pieces—a duck, a dog, or a fish. Old-timers whittled everything from men on the gallows to navigators with sextants to Liberty on her throne. Nor did they forget the sailboat, sails and all, in its many forms—yawls, clippers, and frigates. The era of the American canal, too, produced many specimens of life on the canal: boats, mules, and captains with their warning horns for bridges and locks. And don't forget that the old craftsmen held that their best work was done when they whistled as they whittled!

A Bouquet of Leather Posies

{ 22 }

The results of our research in hobbies and crafts have amazed us many times. Until recently we had thought the leathercraft of Victorian ladies which simulated handcarving on perhaps walnut, mahogany, or rosewood was quite new during the late 1860's and 1870's. Not so; the British Museum has samples from Egypt that date back to 900 B.C. Seventeenth-century ladies of England busied their fingers with this work, imitating clusters of round berries and flowers with which they decorated furniture, plaques, and frames. Little wonder that our own Victorians with their liking for fussy effects revived the craft. The faded, dusty specimens of this once-popular pastime are still to be found adorning picture frames, handkerchief boxes, bracket shelves, and parlor lecterns from which stern and pious grandfathers once read the Sunday morning lesson from the family Bible.

It must be made clear that this almost-forgotten craft is not to be confused with hand-tooling leather for making billfolds or book covers. The work we are concerned with here was more three-dimensional; flowers, leaves, and grapes were made in the manner of waxwork. Craftsmen in wax cut their forms from sheet wax and molded them into shapes; workers in leather did likewise. Some colored their flowers, stems, and leaves with wood stain to make carved effects, others gilded them, and a few painted them red, blue or green. Colored specimens were more often used in shadow boxes; in fact, we have yet to find colored work not encased and protected in this manner. At least such protection must have solved the annoying problem of dusting with something more commodious than a small camel's hair brush.

The most important tools needed are a pair of sharp scissors and a sharp knife, similar to those found in the X-acto knife kits sold in supply shops. Modern craftsmen think it best to make paper patterns of flower petals and leaves, as was the practice in making wax flowers, and to lay these patterns out on the leather and follow around them with the knife. However, a woman may prefer to use scissors. Before leather of any kind is cut, it should be soaked for a minute or two in water and then laid out flat between pieces of cardboard with a weight on top until it is nearly dry. It will then lie flat and be easy to cut.

Perhaps, if you have been dabbling with wax flower-making, you will have some paper patterns that may be applied to leather. The old-time workers in wax always preserved any paper flower patterns that they cut, for future use or for lending to friends engaged in the same hobby.

Also, old-time makers of leather flowers, fruits, and nuts used comparatively simple things: glue, sizing, gold paint, varnish, oil colors, tacks, wire, and thread. Naturally, the basic raw material was leather; this was in the form of thin sheepskin, chamois, or even discarded kid gloves. Today the hobby shop can supply leather in at least one form, and there is always the local chain store or paint shop for pieces of chamois skin.

There are many techniques and variations in this leather flower and fruit craft, particularly in coloring leaves and flowers. Where aniline dyes are to be used it is, of course, advisable to have leathers as close to white as possible. As a matter of fact, all large craft stores carry leather in different thicknesses and in a number of common colors such as green, blue, and red. Therefore, if roses, as an example, are to be modeled in leather, you may purchase red leather for the blossoms and green for the leaves.

If you would like delicate colors or shades not available at the hobby store, then you must color or dye the leather yourself. This is not a hard chore. Naturally, white leather is colored most easily. If ordinary chamois is dyed, the color is apt to be a bit disappointing because of the natural color of the leather. It helps to soak chamois for several hours in a full-strength solution of Clorox. Thorough washing with plenty of warm, clean water will then be necessary in order to remove the last traces of chlorine. Place the chamois in the dye bath while it is still wet and leave it there for the period specified on the package of dyestuff. The rules for dyeing fabrics also apply to dyeing leather. The leather should, first of all, be soaked in warm water for about fifteen minutes.

Some workers painted finished flowers, leaves, and fruit with colored varnishes or enamels. Thus woodcarving is imitated by repeated applications of walnut, maple, or mahogany varnish over a suitable base. Naturally this varnish not only colors the leather but also stiffens it after drying. Many old-time workers painted their finished work with bronze or gold.

To make leaves more realistic, you may vein them after they are cut to shape. To do this use the blunt end of a large darning needle as a pencil, applying it to the top side of the leaf with as much pressure as possible while the leaf is still moist and lying flat. The lines or veins so scored should be gone over repeatedly.

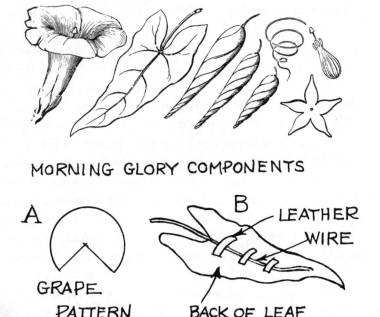

MORNING GLORY COMPONENTS

A   B   LEATHER
              WIRE

GRAPE
PATTERN   BACK OF LEAF

55. Components of a morning glory and the technique employed in making leaves and grapes in leather.

Leather is shapeless and cannot be tooled so that it will hold its shape. Therefore, after leaves are cut and stained, either with an oak, walnut, or other wood stain, or with a dye to give them high color, they must be stiffened. As a sizing or stiffening preparation, some workers used ordinary starch, some copal varnish. The worker today will find water-white varnish which is transparent, white shellac, clear varnish, or plastic varnish available. One coat is usually quite sufficient.

After your preparation has dried, modeling and forming begins along with the installation of wire stems for the leaves (55). Since the back of the leaves will not show in the finished work, adhesive tape, model-airplane or other cements may be used to attach the wire which, in turn, may be painted green or brown with ordinary enamel.

Iron wire, such as is sold on small spools at the hardware counter, is recommended for stems of both leaves and flowers. Individual stems are attached to main stems by the simple device of twisting one around the other. All of these joints are later covered with green crêpe paper wrapped in narrow strips around the main stem. This serves not only to hide the joints but also to increase the size of the main stem. If the shade of the paper does not match that of the green enamel used over the wire stems, apply a coat of green enamel to cover the paper. Twist the wire as tightly as possible at the joints to avoid bumpiness.

After you have stiffened flower petals and leaves with one of the preparations mentioned, it is comparatively easy to give them some shape and form. Lay the prepared blanks on a small bag filled with sand and work them into shape by pressing them with a tool that has a ball-shaped end. This tool is made by soldering a quarter-inch brass ball or ball bearing to the end of an eight-inch brass rod.

Fabricating flowers is not as difficult as you might think. Wherever possible, the whole set of petals (55) should be cut out of a single piece of leather. This makes for sturdy fabrication because the petals won't need to be cemented or glued together to form flowers. The calyx, too, may be cut in one piece for the sake of simplicity. Both the petals and the calyx should have a hole pierced in their exact centers, through which to slip the petals and then the calyx over the wire stem. The calyx is then glued or cemented to the base of the petals and the assembly held to the wire by a drop of airplane cement. After the crêpe-paper strip is wound around the stem of the flowers, still another drop or two of cement is applied to strengthen the joint.

The pistils or filaments of flowers are made of starched or waxed thread of a suitable color. The little knobs at their ends may be formed by re-

56. A small bracket shelf for statuary decorated with leather grape vine and grapes. (From Jones and Williams' *Making Household Elegancies*)

peated dipping in wax. Melted colored candles often supply the needed colors for pistils.

If you are accustomed to painting with oil, don't overlook the possibility of decorating flowers this way, especially when solid colors should not be used. Oil paints can be applied over any of the stiffening agents suggested.

Finally assembled, your group of flowers or fruit may be given a last coat of varnish, enamel, or plastic. The plastic material sold in spray cans is excellent for this. Otherwise, you will have to paint the whole with colored enamel, bronze, oak, walnut, cherry, maple, or mahogany varnish using a small camel's hair brush.

The grouping of your flowers or cluster of fruit depends largely on where it is to be used. If for a glass-covered shadow box, you may hold the ends of wire stems to the wooden backboard with thumbtacks. After these are installed, cement small pieces of lichen moss in place to cover them. Then you are able to bend the stems of the flowers as you see fit to form a group. Follow the same procedure if you want to mount the flowers in a glass dome.

In the last century ladies made convincing bunches of grapes by simply gluing their skivers of leather over marbles, the seams skillfully hidden when the individual grapes were assembled into a bunch. Grape coverings were cut in the shape shown in 55A. First the marble was covered with glue and when this was tacky, the leather was padded around it. A rather long piece of heavy, colored string was glued to the leather to serve as a stem for assembling the grapes into a bunch. Only small bunches of grapes were tied together in this manner. The central stem to which the grapes were tied was usually a small twig from a tree or bush. Stain and then varnish were applied later.

Design in Yarns & Flosses: Swedish Embroidery

{ 23 }

Swedish embroidery is centuries old and uses the simplest basic stitch imaginable; it can be mastered by anyone, even though she has never held a needle or worn a thimble. It has many names, its origins are varied and its adaptations range from ·the most elementary to the most intricate. Whether called Swedish embroidery, Swedish darning, Japanese darning, tacking stitch, darning, double darning, *pessante,* pattern darning, damask darning—all use a running stitch, picking up one or two threads at regular intervals to make the pattern. Naturally, it is necessary to work with a fabric woven so as to produce rows of threads which can be picked up easily.

Huck toweling is the easiest material for the beginner to use because of its weave. It comes in two distinct types: one in white only, coarsely woven and of the type made years ago which is suitable for all-over designs that completely cover the background material; the other is the new huck toweling which is fine in texture, and comes in colors ranging from the pastels to the pure, deep shades so popular now in decoration. These are good for border designs of the simple tacking or running stitch or of more intricate pattern.

The designs may be worked in yarn, six-strand embroidery floss, or Perle cotton floss, depending on the pattern, proposed use, and also the type of huck toweling. One word of caution here: be certain that the huck toweling and working yarn or floss are all colorfast. It is discouraging to find on the first laundering that one or the other runs, thus ruining the design.

The relatively coarse, white huck toweling has been used for a good many years as background material for Swedish embroidery worked in wool. Illustrated is a handbag done by one of the authors (cxii) using 4-ply yarn in red and black. This coarse huck toweling is not easy to find nowadays, since the huck in demand is of finer weave which will not take heavy yarn. You must be certain that the yarn will pass through the vertical threads without trouble. This needlework challenges the artistic and inventive mind, for hundreds of designs can be worked up from the two basic stitches, the running stitch and the loop, as illustrated in 57. A study of the illustration and a simple explanation may help.

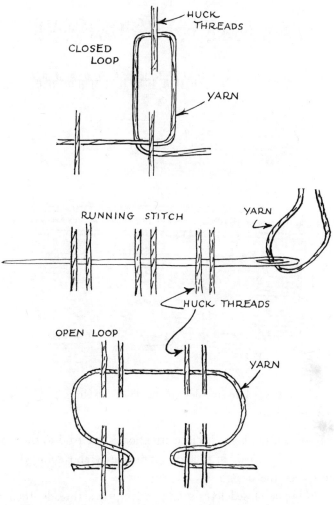

57. The two basic stitches used in Swedish embroidery. See text.

First let us consider the running or, as it is sometimes called, the tacking stitch. In huck toweling the right and wrong sides are not alike. On the working side, the weave is much more noticeable and easy to follow; therefore, always remember to work on the side that has the most prominent threads. Sets of two yarns each go vertically across the material. When working the running stitch, two yarns are picked up by the needle, then the next two immediately adjacent, and so on across.

CXI. Effective designs for huck toweling.

A word of caution here: if close attention is not paid to the work, it is possible to pick up a pair in the row immediately above and thus destroy the symmetry of the design.

In working the closed loop stitch, pick up two threads, then pick up the two immediately above, but point the needle to the right instead of to the left. Next, pick up the *first* pair, again working toward the left. A little practice will make this very simple.

An open loop stitch differs only in that you pick up a pair, then a pair immediately above, to the left for another group, and then a pair of stitches immediately below, working toward the left at all times. With these simple basic stitches in combination, any number of effective designs may be worked out, even by a beginner. As a matter of fact, even the most complicated designs are made by these same stitches.

A word about the needle. A blunt needle such as is used for needlepoint, available at any notion counter, is easier to work with than a needle with a sharp point. The type of embroidery material determines the size and thickness of the needle.

Of course, any real needlewoman is always glad to have people look at the back of her handiwork (and they invariably do!). When starting, do not use a knot. Instead, on the wrong side, make a close running stitch toward the starting point, a small back stitch to hold it, and then put the thread or yarn through to the front or right side.

When starting on articles which will have hems, put a knot under the hem. At the end of the thread fasten by back stitching, with fine stitches to fasten securely before cutting. You must not carry threads across long spaces to start new designs, as this means untidy work on the opposite side.

Experience will help in deciding the length of thread necessary in making motifs or designs so that a minimum of fastening is necessary. Too long a thread will result in "fuzzing" or unwinding of the strands of yarn or floss before it is used up.

With a practice piece of material and floss, work out the pattern as follows: Pick up 10 threads across, *pick up 1 directly above, 1 directly above that, 4 threads over (working to left), 1 down, over 9*. Repeat from * to end of row. The second row above starts with 9 threads, * 1 directly above, up 1, over 5, down 1, down 1, over 8*. Repeat from * to end of row. Third row: pick up 8 threads, * 1 up, 1 up, over 6, down 1, down 1, over 7*. Repeat from *. Fourth row: over 7, * up 1, up 1, over 7, down 1, down 1, over 6 *. Repeat from * Fifth row: over 6, * 1 up, 1 up, over 8, down 1, down 1, over 5 *. Repeat from * to end of row.

A number of simple designs which can be used for borders is illustrated in CXI. The last pattern in this picture is the one described above.

In planning all work it is wise to see that the pattern is "centered." Most workers (not the beginner, but one who has mastered at least the simple stitches and wishes to go on to slightly more difficult work) count threads on the toweling, dividing the total number of threads by the number of the threads in the motif. This basic design will be repeated as many times as necessary to form the whole pattern. Counting will determine the placing of the motifs. Sometimes it is best to have a motif "straddle" the center line, sometimes to have one on each side of the center, depending on the size of the motif and the amount of area which is to be covered. An example

CXII. Handbag done with Swedish embroidery worked in red-and-black wool. Coarse white huck toweling provides the background.

may be helpful. Let us take the last motif as shown in CXI. You will notice that it shows a balanced pattern. This, incidentally, is very effective and certainly will not tax the ingenuity of even the most inexperienced needle-woman.

If you are not inclined to make your own designs, there are a number of sources for designs which can be used on huck toweling. Mildred V. Krieg of Riverside, Illinois, has a series of booklets containing designs which can be purchased direct or through the Niagara Textile Company, Lockport, New York, at 25 cents each. The Niagara Textile Company makes a complete line of handsome huck toweling in a wide range of colors suitable for many needs. Most pattern companies that handle handwork patterns issue groups of designs for Swedish Embroidery or Swedish Darning, as it is often called.

Swedish embroidery on huck toweling can be used in a variety of ways, depending on texture of toweling and type of working material. To name a few: guest towels, aprons, place mats, handbags, knitting bags, curtains, dresser scarves. All are durable and decorative and can be made quickly.

Any design, simple or intricate, can be made more effective and individual by using two or more colors in combination. And it's really fun to experiment! Most handwork requires skill and training, but this type of embroidery can be mastered by the novice in a very short time. The experienced needlewoman, too, can find enjoyment and an outlet for her creative skill and artistry. It is little wonder that this type of embroidery has lived on for generations.

INDEX

stereoscopic pictures, developing, 54
  enlarging, 55
  printing, 54–55
  taking, 54
Swedish embroidery, basic stitches in,
    213
  borders for, 214
  closed loop stitch in, 214–215
  designs for, 217
  huck toweling for, 212–213
  materials for, 212
  needle for, 215
  open loop stitch in, 214
  pattern for, 215
  running stitch in, 214
  techniques of, 215–217

tapestry needlework, 73. *See also* Berlin
    wool work.
Tilton, S. W., 198
tinselwork, 38, 40
tinware, covers for, 100
tinware decorating, antique effect in,
    108–111
  brush strokes for, 111
  by freehand painting, 106–108
  designs for, 111
  japanned effect in, 106–107, 113,
    118–120
  with stencils, 107, 118–121
tinware making, equipment for, 100
  materials for, 96
  preparation for, 96
  with sheet tin, 99
  soldering in, 100–106
  with tin cans, 96, 99–100
  tools for, 96, 99–100
transparencies, finishing effects for, 32
  for folding screens, 36–38
  how to hang, 31
  hanging-type, adhesive tape for, 28
    colored inks for, 28
    decalcomania transfers for, 29–30
    ground-glass effect in, 28
    materials for, 27, 28, 29
    oil colors for, 28

    ribbon for, 28
    spatter technique for, 29
    stained-glass-window effect in, 28–
      31
    steel engravings for, 31–35
    tools for, 27
  mounting, 26
  tinselwork in, 38, 40

wall paper, block-printed, 47–48
  designing, 46–47
  early American, 41–42
  stenciling, 45
  stencils, equipment for, 43–44
    materials for, 43–44
    multicolor effect for, 44
    single-color effect for, 43
wall-paper designs, for folding screens,
    38
  subjects for, 46–47
Waring, Janet, 47
wax flowers, materials for making, 157–
    158, 161
  mounting, 167
  techniques of making, 159–167
  tools for making, 161–162, 164
  use of paraffin for, 158
  wax for, coloring, 158–159
    making, 157
    melting, 159
    painting, 167
    types of, 167
wax fruit, casting mold for, 152–154
  making mold for, 147–148, 150
  materials for, 147
  tools for, 147
welding. *See* smithing, techniques of.
whittling, decorations for, 205
  products of, 200, 205
  techniques of, 201–205
  tools for, 200, 201, 203, 204
  woods for, 200, 201
Williams, Henry T., 26, 29, 30, 40, 59,
    61, 75, 160, 161, 210
winter bouquets, 138, 141–146